Jon does not shy away from the big issues facing the church. In his previous book he tackled the dehumanizing marginalization of women in the church. Here he tackles the equally debilitating doctrine that has rendered the church ineffective, and reinstates the deeply biblical understanding of the priesthood of every believer. A courageous book that ought to be read with an open heart.

— **Alan Hirsch**
The Forgotten Ways, Re-Jesus,
www.theforgottenways.org

What can we say? The cover of this book says it all! Hebrews talks about God shaking everything that can be shaken, and this volume by Jon Zens goes right to the foundations of our current church system, based upon the role of the "Pastor." This book discovers more than mere cracks in the foundations, but rather finds serious flaws in a man-made system that substitutes human traditions for the presence and power of God. You may not like the way that Jon challenges the pastor-led system of modern church (modern in the sense that it is all most Christians have known for the past 1700 years), but you will find it hard to argue with his conclusions.

— **Tony & Felicity Dale**
founders of House2House & authors of
Simply Church, Small Is Big!

Jon Zens has written one of the most important books of the 21st century. If you thought *Pagan Christianity* was controversial, think again. Jon's book demonstrates beyond dispute that the clergy-system (in the form of the modern pastorate) is not only unbiblical but also contrary to the headship of Jesus Christ.

I hope that every Christian reads this volume with an open heart and mind, especially those who deem themselves "leaders" in the body of Christ. I applaud Jon for his courage in adding another Scripture-based book to help foment the growing revolution that God has begun today—a revolution designed to give His church back to His beloved Son.

— **Frank Viola**
Revise Us Again, From Eternity to Here,
Jesus Manifesto, Reimagining Church
and Pagan Christianity.
www.ptmin.org

As a pastor of the largest evangelical congregation in northwestern Oklahoma, one might think I could possibly be threatened by Jon's premise in this book. How can I be? *The Pastor Has No Clothes* is thoroughly biblical and a wake up call to all of us pastors who have forgotten that every believer in Christ is a priest unto Him and that the only authority within the church is Christ's.

— **Wade Burleson**
Emmanuel Baptist Church,
Enid, Oklahoma

I owe Jon a debt of love. It was because I posted his "Clergy" video that I lost my pastoral job! In his compelling new book, *The Pastor Has No Clothes,* Jon describes how the current structure of the institutional church has created over time an unhealthy balance in the body of Christ. He challenges us to look at the pastoral system in light of the way the New Testament early church functioned. A must-read and insightful book!

— **Joseph Hunter**
former pastor, Tennessee

Jon Zens, one of the original voices of the worldwide house church movement, has gathered together in one volume some of the tastiest of his writings about the "pastorate." This book will be tough reading for those whose livelihood depends on Jon being *wrong*, but a welcome breath of fresh air for those who are redefining success in ways, which cannot be measured by formulas, but by the presence of the Messiah Jesus in a local community of people—the *ekklesia* no less. His writings about the pastorate remind me of the story of the Titanic. This ship was a structure so large that its builders claimed vigorously that it could not sink, but as we all know it did not take long for it to go under after all. This is also how the pastorate is seen today— unchangeable, untouchable and unsinkable, a subject for the academy but not for the local *ekklesia*. Jon's writings are not unlike the iceberg that caused so much damage under the water line of the Titanic—they have removed the untouchable status that has kept this topic hidden, and now the pastorate is coming under the scrutiny of the body of Christ. The destruction that the pastorate has done to those who are involved in it, including family and churches alike, is well documented, but up to now ignored. Jon does a good job in bringing this tale of destruction to our notice. We do not have to agree with everything that Jon says, but we have to receive these writings as timely additions to the deconstruction of the edifice of the monolithic church system, which has held the *ekklesia* back from full expression. I highly recommend this book for your serious consideration.

— **Douglas Gerald Heffernan**
Overseer, Celtic Prayer Centre,
Cork, Ireland

A striking and thorough explication of the pastor-dominated tradition, this book addresses the fine points of the pastor-cen- tric paradigm, uncovering numerous ways the headship of Jesus Christ is inadvertently usurped amid a Christian culture of hero- worship a religious celebrity. For those who have ears to hear, Jon Zens' words have the ability to breathe new hope and fire into the lives of those dedicated souls who love the church, but have for far too long been carrying the weight of it on their shoulders. Like everything else that comes from the pen of this brother, *The Pastor Has No Clothes* is another must read.

— **Dr. Stephanie Bennett**
Associate Professor of Communication and
Media Studies, Palm Beach Atlantic University
W. Palm Beach, Florida

Jon Zens was pursuing what some today call the "organic" Christian life when the rest of us still thought the term related to carrots. He is a pioneering prophetic teacher in the best sense of those terms. *The Pastor Has No Clothes* is classic Zens: the impeccable research of a scholar, a passion for the supremacy of scripture over tradition, a lover's heart for Truth in scripture, all motivated from a care for God's people that burns like fire in a prophet's bones. This work is uncompromising in conviction yet absent is the untempered and antagonistic zealotry that can so often accompany writings of this nature. Make no mistake. Though irenic in spirit, the truth Jon presents does what truth is supposed to do: it cuts. Vested interests will feel the sting. Those oppressed by vested interests will feel the liberty.

—**Stephen Crosby**
author of *Praise, Worship and the Presence of God—
A Better Way to Worship: A New Covenant Perspective,*
North Carolina

If the Western nations are to see movements of simple church multiplication that effectively reap a harvest for the Kingdom, then we must get back to disciple-making and the "one another-ing" of being church that Jesus envisioned. Here, Jon helps us get a handle on one of the major blocks to these good things happening—the "us and them" of the "clergy/laity" divide. *The Pastor Has No Clothes* will help clergy who have left the traditional system to work in missional movements, to detox from "pastor-conditioning," and to assist simple church groups not to "re-invent the wheel" of denominational thinking and practice.

— **Bessie Pereira**
Director, OIKOS Australia
www.oikos.org.au

The gospel was to form a New Covenant body of believers who related to one another without regard to distinctions. Yet it seems as though modern churches with pastors, elders and deacons, function more like an Old Covenant hierarchy of high priests and Levites performing for the on-looking worshipers. I've been reading Jon's articles on pastors and church leaders since the '80s and they have had a profound impact on my thinking. At one time I was "the pastor," but now I rejoice to be in a fellowship where we relate equally rather than having one man or group as a ruling class. Jon's articles appear more relevant than ever!

— **Timothy King**
www.restorationgj.com
Colorado

In this book Jon Zens has taken dead aim at the most sacred cow of all within institutional Christianity—the Pastorate. He does this with a precise biblical scholarship, and with a keen eye for details. No stone is left unturned in this study of this most unscriptural yet most popular role and practice. Jon hits the target dead on! Never before have I read such a biblically and experientially accurate treatment of the subject.

— **Milt Rodriguez**
author of *The Priesthood of All Believers,*
The Temple Within & The Butterfly in You

After living the first 30 years of my life as a "lay person" I entered seminary in 1976, graduated with an M.Div. from Fuller

Seminary in 1980 and entered the professional ministry. How I wish I had been able to read Jon Zens' work before I began that part of my journey.

Even when I was a youngster growing up in church I observed something that didn't make sense to me: most people didn't "do anything" as Christians. They just went to church and seemed to devote their efforts to avoiding doing anything wrong but little or nothing beyond that. The "ministering people" were all pastors or missionaries and the rest of us were to support them or become one of them.

Now, after 30 years in the professional ministry, growing my last church to a congregation of 2000, I am convinced that the problems I saw as a child were not unique to a particular church or denomination but to a whole system of being and doing church. Somewhere after the first or second century of the church we began to lose the concept and practice of the priesthood of all believers and began to function as if the pastors, then priests, were the ministering people and the only ones capable of either hearing Jesus or responding to Jesus or partnering with Jesus in his work.

For years I battled against these beliefs and practices, assuming that most everyone shared the understanding that what Jesus sought was the priesthood of all believers, and that Jesus was wonderfully present and able to guide, counsel, lead, gift and work through and with all of his followers. But time and again I found my efforts blunted, resisted, thwarted by my position as a "pastor."

It was assumed that I, as a pastor, was somehow closer to God. I was better able to follow God. I was better able to listen to God. I was expected to live a different standard than everyone else. Ultimately I was not even to have friends among the people I served. There was too much professional power imbalance to allow such a thing.

What Jon has done in his exhaustive examination and critique of current belief and practice about the pastor and the church is to pull aside the mystique, and reveal a systemic problem that has crippled the work that Jesus has for his followers to carry out as his friends and co-workers. With quote after quote and article after article Jon has laid bare the awful truth, that we pastors have inserted ourselves between Jesus and his people and, rather than help them listen and follow, we have dulled their hearing and turned them to us rather than to Him.

Whether "lay person" or "clergy person," read what Jon has written and revealed and allow yourself to listen to what you are reading and listen to Jesus at the same time. Jon writes as a prophetic voice to help pastors see the truth and the people to see the truth, to turn from a man-created system and return to a Jesus-led church.

— **John Strong**
once again, a "lay person"
and rejoicing! California

THE PASTOR HAS NO CLOTHES!
MOVING FROM CLERGY-CENTERED CHURCH TO CHRIST-CENTERED EKKLESIA
BY JON ZENS

PUBLISHER'S CATALOGING-IN-PUBLICATION DATA
(provided by Quality Books, Inc.)

Zens, Jon.
   The Pastor Has No Clothes! : Moving from Clergy-Centered Church to Christ-Centered Ekklesia / Jon H. Zens ; foreword by Neil Cole.

   p. cm.
   Includes bibliographical references.
   ISBN 978-0-9827446-4-2

1. Clergy --United States. 2. Christianity --United States --21st century. 3. Christian leadership --Biblical teaching. 4. Leadership --Religious aspects --Christianity. I. Title.

BV652.1 .Z46 2011   253 --dd22
                          2011923485

This volume is printed on acid free paper and meets ANSI Z39.48 standards.

Cover design and layout by: Rafael Polendo (polendo.net)

Printed in the United States of America

Ekklesia Press is a ministry to help authors get published and to publish works that are not deemed "profitable" by the mainstream publishing industry. Our goal is to put works into print that will impact and motivate followers of Christ to fulfill the Great Commission in an ever increasing way.

Ekklesia Press is an extension of www.kingdomcitizenship.org

Ekklesia Press
5015 Poppleton Avenue, #4
Omaha, Nebraska 68106

THE PASTOR HAS NO CLOTHES!
MOVING FROM CLERGY-CENTERED CHURCH
TO CHRIST-CENTERED EKKLESIA

BY JON ZENS

Ekklesia Press

Lincoln, Nebraska

I dedicate this book to

MARV AND JODI ROOT

who have shared their hearts, their home, and their very lives
with us as we pursue Jesus together in a world full of deep hurt.

TABLE OF CONTENTS

James D.G. Dunn highlighted a very serious problem when he noted: "some of the early statements regarding industrial chaplaincies...seemed to imply that the Church was not present in industry unless and until an ordained clergyman became involved on the factory floor." The idea that clergy must be present in order for the church to exist and function is one of the most debilitating assumptions in the body of Christ. Too many in both the church and world believe that you simply can't have church without a clergyperson present.

We allow this most distressing lie to creep into our ways, thus becoming sacred, unchangeable dogma reverently referred to as "the pastor's call" and "ordination." The reality is this: the New Testament says nothing about clergy being different from laity; we are all "the inheritance" (Greek: *kleros*) and we are all God's "people" (Greek: *laos*). We are all a holy priesthood, every one of us. In other words: *the laity are the clergy and the clergy are the laity.* There should be no distinction and separation that we commonly see today among those purporting to be the body of Christ. Instead of a priesthood of all believers, we end up with the *"pewhood"* of the disengaged spectators masquerading as the body.

Early in my Christian life, I was spoon-fed this doctrine of the few who are specially called, ordained and given the position of pastor to lead others. I believed I was one of those special people and went off to seminary to be taught how to serve the church in this "holy calling." I went through the process of licensure and ordination to reinforce this sense of being special. I remember wanting to settle the doctrinal foundation of the positional authority for the pastor once and for all, but was gravely disappointed by a glaring lack of Biblical support. But that didn't deter me for, like my leaders before me, I found support in places where it was not to be found. I assumed much and read my own bias into the text many times over...and no one ever openly questioned it.

This was my life's pattern until one day God finally broke through the clutter in my head with clear and profound truth. When the lie was uprooted and replaced with a truly Biblical worldview it changed *everything*. The implications affect every part of life as a follower of the King.

In reality, we misplace our faith by believing we need a person in charge more than we need the Spirit of God. We doubt that the Spirit is enough to lead a meeting and, instead, place hope in one leader to hear from God as if he or she can tell us what we need to hear. Thus, we bypass any common interaction with the indwelling Spirit of God and with each other. How absurd is it when we trust more in the flesh than the Spirit? In the end, we actually have so little faith in the Great Shepherd to lead us that He has become an absentee king delegating his responsibility to a few. This, of course, is not true. But it is the way we function. Ours is a problem of faith. Plain and simple, we do not believe He is capable or motivated to lead us.

In this thoughtful resource book, Jon Zens hits this issue hard with the following question: "Just think with me for a moment. If the senior pastors of the 1000 largest churches in America resigned tomorrow, what kind of religious chaos would ensue?"

I am very grateful for Jon's mind and pen, a gift to the organic church and the kingdom at large. His *What's With Paul & Women?* is outstanding! This book is equally an intelligent and well-studied contribution to a serious but over-looked issue we need to address as a body. As Jon states, "The point is, in organic meetings *the leadership of the Spirit is fluid and over a period of time involves everyone*. If a group looks to the same person time after time to get things rolling, and provide the essential content of the gathering, then the *living Christ blossoming through all the parts* is soured."

I have been teaching similar ideas for a while now. One of the greatest ironies I encounter is in hearing pastors object that if we actually did church this way they would not enjoy the fulfillment of using their gift in the church. Should everyone else table their gifts so that the pastor can feel good about his own usefulness? This is why Jon comments that, "Those who have had leadership positions in the institutional church must take their ambitions and history of being 'up front' to the cross. They must take their proper place of being just a brother or just a sister among other brothers and sisters. If not, then the group will inevitably revert back to an institutional form, which usurps Jesus' leadership."

Again, this is a faith issue. Trust that the Spirit of Christ wants all of His body being fulfilled and used, even pastors and teachers. Yes, it may be fulfilled in a manner far different than our expectations, but fulfillment is always satisfying. It may be different, but it will not be disappointing.

In the Hans Christian Anderson fable, once the boy speaks up everyone realizes how foolish they have been and the ridiculous parade ends. Jon, though not a child, has nonetheless shouted out very clearly—"the pastor has no clothes!" It is time to stop the parade of vain and self-congratulatory cheers stirred on by some lying scam artist that has come to steal the wealth of the King, and go back to normal life...fully clothed.

— **Neil Cole**
author of *Organic Church* and *Journeys to Significance: Charting a Leadership Course from the Life of Paul*
Long Beach, California
February 2011

In Hans Christian Andersen's folktale *The Emperor's New Clothes* (1837), two unscrupulous weavers promise a pretentious Emperor, who cares only for his own appearance, a new suit of clothes—invisible to those too unfit, stupid, or incompetent—which he proudly wears to the adulation and false praise of his subjects. In fact, he's parading around with nothing on. He continues his farcical behaviors until an innocent child finally cries out, "But he isn't wearing anything at all!" Only then do the masses speak honestly, echoing the child's observation, shamefully admitting their error.

Visible Christianity has been parading its one-leader doctrine since about 250 A.D. Elaborate, bureaucratic religious structures have been and continue to be built around this notion—yet in reality, it is "without clothing" and, at long last, a number of people from the pews are beginning to exclaim, "the pastor has no clothes."

However, understand that this book is not about *people*. Rather, I am dealing with a *clergy system* that is a tremendous negative upon persons who have been clothed by it. Frank Viola and George Barna made this clear in their ground-breaking book, *Pagan Christianity*:

> Note that we are using the term pastor to depict the contemporary pastoral office and role, not the specific individual who fills this role. By and large, those who serve in the office of pastor are wonderful people. They are honorable, decent, and very often-gifted Christians who love God and have a zeal to serve His people. But it is the role they fill that both Scripture and church history are opposed to (Tyndale, 2007, p. 106).

Some people view their profession as part of their being and identity as a human being. This holds true for many in the clergy. Thus, if the system they are in is critiqued, they can easily take it personally. *But the problems rest in a system—a system that deeply affects the "clergy" and "laity" who find themselves in it.*

In 1969 my wife and I were planning to go to India and help run an orphanage. I was planning to go to seminary one semester, and then leave the country. Our visa was turned down and I ended up finishing seminary in 1972. So I know about the pastor system, and was in it for a brief period.

In 1977 my journey took a decided turn. From 1964 until then, I was in religious traditions that were camped around the Law. Now, I began to see that believers were under the New Covenant in a living relationship with Jesus Christ–led by His Spirit, not driven by the Letter of the Mosaic Law or any legal system.

As I came face-to-face with Jesus' "new command" to love one another as he had loved us on the cross, I wrote "As I Have Loved You: The Starting Point of Christian Obedience" in 1980 where I consider the 58 "one-another(s)"in the New Testament.[1] I realized that our whole approach to church was incorrectly skewed. *We were elevating that for which there was no basis in the New Testament—one person behind a pulpit—and failing to practice that for which there was plentiful evidence— one-another body ministry.*

These and additional studies then led me to write, "Building Up the Body: One Man or One Another?" in 1981, an article that got me into a lot of hot water back then.[2] I knew it was very controversial and I asked for feedback by sending a rough draft to around 100 people, many of them pastors, before publishing it. What input I received was incorporated into the manuscript, but I heard from only a few pastors, and their comments appealed to religious traditions, without any basis from Scripture.

In 1982, I published the little booklet, *The Pastor.* I had come across a short article by Frank Owen in a Southern Baptist publication that tried to defend the notion that "an orderly church needs one pastor." I responded to this common opinion with what seemed to me to be New Testament perspectives. This booklet over the years apparently helped many folks, and deeply impacted Frank Viola around 1998. (Frank's 2008 book with George Barna, *Pagan Christianity*, traces the historical roots of the modern pastoral office among other Protestant traditions).

By 1995, my heart was greatly burdened by the pervasive chasm between "leaders" and "congregation." In all the various pieces of literature that crossed my desk, I kept seeing remarks like, "Finally a commentary accessible to both clergy and laity." This, coupled with the rise of "Clergy Appreciation Day" in the Promise Keepers' movement, moved me to write, "The Clergy/Laity Distinction: Help or Hindrance to the Body of Christ?"[3]

In January 2011, in response to a sister's comments on Facebook, I wrote "The New Testament Is Plural (Us) Not Singular (Me)," which seemed well received by the Body. Being short and to the point, it serves as an appropriate *Prelude* to articles that follow in this book.

HarperOne released Eugene Peterson's *The Pastor: A Memoir* in February, 2011. Since he is a well-respected evangelical leader and long-time pastor, it seemed well-timed to include "Romancing the Pastorate," which is my response to this book in light of the issues covered in the other essays.

I trust that these three articles from the past, plus the three new essays, "The NT Is Plural (Us) Not Singular (Me)," "The Pastor Has No Clothes!" and "Romancing the Pastorate" will help you in your journey with Jesus. It very much seems we are living in fascinating times when the traditional wineskins are bursting, and new wine is gushing forth from the One who miraculously supplied superb drink at a wedding in Cana.

ENDNOTES:

1. Jon Zens, "As I Have Loved You: The Starting Point of Christian Obedience," *Baptist Reformation Review*, 9:2, Summer, 1980. (*BRR*'s name was changed to *Searching Together* in mid-1982).

2. Jon Zens, "Building Up the Body: One Man or One Another?" *Baptist Reformation Review*, 10:2, Summer, 1981.

3. Jon Zens, "The Clergy/Laity Distinction: Help or Hindrance to the Body of Christ?" *Searching Together*, 23:4, Winter, 1995.

As folks listen to the majority of local and media Bible teachers, most do not catch the fact that Christ's body is missing from the New Testament presentation they are hearing. More often than not the approach taken is entirely individualistic, attempting to answer the question: "How can Christ help me live the Christian life?" However, the NT was not written to individuals but to groups of believing people in various cities and regions. This does not come across in English translations because the word "you" in the Greek can be singular or plural. For example, the "you" in "Christ in you, the hope of glory," is plural, and implies a view of the Body of Christ.

Think about it. The NT letters were sent to *ekklesias* (assemblies)— "when you come together as an *ekklesia*." Even the letter sent to an individual—Philemon—has a corporate (body) dimension to it—"to Apphia our sister, and to Archippus our fellow soldier, and to the *ekklesia* in your house."

This is a crucial missing element in most of today's Bible teaching. We ought to seriously consider that The Lord intended our lives to be lived out among each other in local community, not in isolation. Consider how upside-down we are in our modern practice. The NT has at least 58 "one-another(s)" that are *meaningless* without the reality of close, deep local inter-personal relationships. The call to be longsuffering and forbearing with others makes no real sense without day-to-day involvement that simply does not and cannot take place by seeing people for a few hours a week at agenda-controlled religious meetings with stifled communications.

In practice, though, where do we most commonly put the emphasis on what people call "church"? It pretty much revolves around "the pastor." He is the one with the training, the ordination, the assumed leadership "vision," and the stock sermon repertoire. Without a "pastor" people will generally conclude that you don't have a church. So, if a "pastor" leaves a church, then a general crisis ensues because he has to be replaced and quickly.

What have we done? We have elevated a mere traditional concept—that there must be a "pastor" to lead the church— for which there is not a shred of evidence in the NT. By doing this, most church structures suppress the life of Jesus coming to expression through the 58 "one-another(s)"that are clearly in the NT. Then, since the "one-another" perspectives are pushed into the background, the "pastor" spends much of his time helping the flock live the Christian life *as individuals*.

It is apparent that, in the NT, Christ's life in each believer comes to expression as they gather in open meetings and edify each other (1 Corinthians 14:26). The NT knows nothing of the "worship services" as practiced now. In early church gatherings there was no one person, or group, "up-front" leading the time together. It was a body meeting led by the Holy Spirit as an expression of Jesus Christ.

What are we doing? We bring individuals together who haven't seen each other since last Sunday (maybe) to sing a few over-used songs, lay some money in a plate, listen to a practiced pastoral prayer, hear a rehearsed sermon, and then return to home to isolated meals and mindless television watching. "Church services" climax with the sermon and perhaps an altar call, for those of the slightly more evangelical persuasions. Otherwise, church attendees simply go through whatever is ordained in the weekly church bulletin without necessarily having an ounce of loving commitment to anyone. Individuals and families sit in the pews week after week who are dysfunctioning in stress-filled pressure cookers of bad jobs, financial distress, relationship collapses and generally living lives of lies, despair and self-destruction, yet they routinely fall through the cracks of the organized, pastor-led church machinery.

Early believers gathered together in a way where *all* could be part of an expression of Christ on earth and to their local community. For all intents and purposes, we now come to "church" to see one person religiously function and hear a sermon often reflecting fallen worldly values and concerns. Do you see the disconnect? The former is Christ flowing like living water from His people in a life of interdependence; the latter is institutional and fosters inappropriate dependence on one part: "the pastor."

Consider the matter of repentance. Generally this subject is approached individualistically—"What do I need to repent of in my Christian life?" This is certainly an important dimension of the Christian life. But in Christ's words to the *ekklesias* in Revelation 2 & 3 we see that he called the whole body of believers in a city to repent of various sins. This is *we*-repentance not *me*-repentance. When have you ever heard of a body of believers repenting for anything?

Indeed, the *ekklesia* consists of unique individuals. But the Lord's building of his *ekklesia* through these individuals finds its fullest manifestation in *togetherness*. For sure, many believers find depth, growth and joyous existence in Christ even in periods of isolation or wilderness experience. But the overall picture shows Christ purposing for his vine-life to be fruitful in each and every branch, for the health and growth of the whole plant.

Our life is just a vapor. Are we going to expend our energies oiling religious machines or pursuing life—"Christ in us the hope of glory"?

(For further reflection on this theme and related ones see the author's *A Church Building Every ½ Mile: What Makes American Christianity Tick?*)

"*In time, all institutions follow a similar pattern. They begin as fresh movements, new and exciting, abundant with vision and creativity. But in order to survive, a movement must develop structural strength—mission statement, doctrinal distinctives, leadership structure, decision-making processes.*

Vigorous change takes place during this organizational phase as a seedling becomes established, sinking its roots and spreading its branches. Staff are hired, budgets are created, policies are instituted, goals and objectives are set, property is purchased. As the organization matures it becomes a source of security for its employees. Health insurance, vacation pay, cost of living raises, retirement benefits are negotiated. Gradually the mission shifts from the founding visionaries to hired employees and with each subsequent ring of management the passion that originally inspired the movement becomes slightly diluted. Marketing, management, and funding consume increasing amounts of organizational energy. With its own sturdy root system, it now commands its fair share of sunlight and space on the forest floor.

By the time the organization enters the institutional phase of its development, it is fully vested in its own self-preservation. Instead of a movement spending itself on behalf of a noble cause, it has become a respectable institution consumed with preserving its own viability and legacy. It may still use the same stirring language of its past movement days, and it may still perform important work, but it spends the lion's share of its energy on buildings, communication systems, internal politics and self-promotion to ensure its longevity. Good stewardship demands its preservation. It is the way of all institutions."

— **Bob Lupton**
"Cycle of Life," September, 2010,
http://fcsministries.orgurban-perspectives/page/2/

THE PASTOR HAS NO CLOTHES!

"THE BODY IS NOT ONE PART..." (1 CORINTHIANS 12:14A) WE'VE MADE "CHURCH" REST ON ONE PERSON

In 1 Corinthians 12, Paul discussed the metaphoric reality that there is only one body of Christ, but that this body has many parts with each individual part benefiting the entire Spiritual body (v. 7). In order for any composite or physical body (made up of differing, interrelated components) to be healthy—especially the spiritual body of Christ—*all the parts must be functioning.*

Is it any wonder that the body of Christ is so sick? The too-common daily dysfunctional picture that we portray to a watching world comes down to this: *the inception, growth, health and future of the church rests entirely on the shoulders of one person—the pastor.* We make "church" dependent on one part, and thereby have flatly contradicted Paul's inspired observation that "the body is *not* one part."

Is that an exaggeration? I don't think so. Listen to what those who advocate and defend a one-pastor system say about the centrality of "the pastor" and his pulpit:

» The pastor has the "master role" in "an occupation distinguished from the occupational role of other persons" (Samuel W. Blizzard, Princeton Theological Seminary, quoted in *Neurotics in the Church*, Robert James St. Clair, Revell, 1963, p. 24).

» "Eight ways to view pastoral leadership as the primary ministry in the church" (Description of lead article, "Pastor For Life," *Ministry*, July/August, 2010, p. 3).

» "The local church pastor is key—absolutely central—to everything we are and do as a church. It's a truth that's been expressed so many times that perhaps it's acquired the air of a cliché. But, nevertheless, it expresses reality"

(Jan Paulsen, "A Message of Appreciation," *Ministry*, July/August, 2010, p. 4).

» "The pastor is the *leading* officer of a congregation" (Reformed Presbyterian Book of Church Government, Chapter 4, paragraph 3, cited in the *Covenanter Witness*, August 30, 1972).

» "*The Pastor is a Gift to the Church....* he is a Pastor by divine ordination, altogether superior to any human planning.... The Pastor is the one who *divides* the truth to the flock, or assembly, over whom God hath appointed him" (I.M. Haldeman, *How to Study the Bible*, Revell, 1904, p. 396).

» "I do not care for the term *Chief Pastor*. Possibly the direct article, 'the' pastor, 'the' bishop, 'the' elder, is sufficient designation for the pastor of any particular church, while other elders, pastors, bishops are simply referred to without the direct article (p. 12).... I hold that a church, if it is large enough to afford and needs more than one pastor, must look upon one of these pastors as the pastor, the spokesman for the other pastors and for the church (p. 13)" (E.W. Johnson, *Sovereign Grace Message*, March, 1974).

» "Such preaching plays a central part in pastoral work, for it is the main means by which the people of God are built up in faith (p. 72).... It is through the preaching of the Word that the people of God will grow in their knowledge of God (p. 27)" (Herbert Carson, *Hallelujah! Christian Worship*, Evangelical Press, 1980).

» "Much of what happens in our worship services is standardized" by the "ordained eldership." "The worshipping congregation is to be actively involved in whatever happens in worship." This can happen, the author suggests, by (1) taking notes during the sermon and (2) having an open Bible (Leonard J. Coppes, *Are Five Points Enough? The Ten Points of Calvinism*, Reformation Educational Foundation, 1980, p. 179).

» "In its regular [church] life, the official ministry is central" to Puritan John Owen (p. 21). "Puritan attention when discussing gifts was dominated by their interest in the ordained ministry, and hence in those particular gifts, which qualify a man for ministerial office, and questions about other gifts to other persons were rarely raised (p. 15)" (J.I. Packer, "The Puritans & Spiritual Gifts," *"Profitable for Doctrine & Reproof" —The 1967 Westminster Papers*).

» "The core issue…is a need for the development of, and commitment to, a culture of viewing pastoral leadership as the primary ministry in the denomination's structure" (Ivan C. Blake, "Pastor for Life," *Ministry*, July/August, 2010, p. 8).

» "Preaching is presented [in Rom. 10:14] as essential to evangelism and salvation…. The answer is found in v. 15, 'How beautiful are the feet of those who preach the Gospel'—the answer is a preacher" (Charles E. McLain, "The Centrality of Preaching," *Calvary Baptist Theological Journal*, Fall, 1987, p. 22).

» "The interest and value of worship, as conducted in most churches, depend chiefly on the pastor. The service is almost wholly led by him" (Hezekiah Harvey, *The Pastor* [1879], Backus Books, 1982, pp. 27-28).

» Concerning tax breaks for the clergy: "In plain language, 'If you are ordained, commissioned, or licensed and meet the following three tests, the IRS will generally consider you a minister. You: must administer the sacraments, conduct worship services, and perform services in the control, conduct, or maintenance of a church.' David Epstein, a tax attorney and author on 'clergy' tax, while appearing as a guest a on 'Money Matters' radio broadcast stated that one would only have to meet the ordination or licensing requirement and any two of four other requirements: 1. That you lead religious worship. 2. That you administer the sacraments. 3. You have administrative or management functions. 4. Are considered a spiritual leader within your church.' Other interpretations of the relative tax codes cause even greater concern: 'To sustain self-employment status, a minister would need to convince the IRS that no one has right to control either the method or the means by which his ministry is conducted. This might also include the authority to unilaterally discontinue the regular service of a local church.' In light of the word 'unilateral' and 'his ministry' certainly suggest that in order to qualify for this status, the 'minister' must be in total control of everything that goes on in the church. Whether that is the intended interpretation is not the point.... The IRS's method for determining who qualifies as a 'minister,' therefore, is rooted less in legislative caprice than in the distorted church patterns from which the government has derived its rules and regulations" (Alan Allison, "Render Not Unto Caesar The Things That Are God's," *Searching Together*, 26:3-4, Fall-Winter, 1998).

» "If you have a strong pulpit, you're going to have a strong church, no matter if everything else is lacking.... Preaching has got to be there or people are not going to come" (Harold Ockenga, "Chairman of the Board," *Christianity Today*, Nov. 6, 1981, p. 27).

» "The government of the Church is Presbyterian: Ministers or teaching Elders are the highest officers, and among these there is perfect parity of power" (*The Reformed Presbyterian Testimony*, XXIII:3 cited in *Blue Banner of Faith & Life*, April-June, 1959, p. 98).

» Regarding pastor John Smalley's (1734-1820) entrance into the church building: "It was doubtless with assurance born of the reverence with which he was customarily regarded, that by stamping upon the meeting-house doorway floor

Smalley made known to his congregation the moment of his arrival, so that members of importance might rise and make him their obeisance as he passed down the center aisle on Sabbath [Sunday] mornings" (Mary Latimer Gambrell, *Ministerial Training in 18th Century New England*, pp. 113-114).

» "HOW TO ADDRESS A PASTOR.... The pastor should not be called by his first name.... At times first names can be fitting and appropriate, but not for your parents, nor for judges, not for law officers, nor for preachers. It is a matter of respect for the position and office. A pastor may be called Bishop, Elder, Pastor, or Brother.... How very true the statement, 'Familiarity breeds contempt.' Refraining from calling a Pastor by his first name does not mean he is more spiritual than his flock, but it does mean he holds the highest office in the church, namely that of God's undershepherd, which demands respect, as seen in Hebrews 13:24" (Dan Cozart, Church Bulletin, Sovereign Grace Baptist Church, Tyler, Texas, January 8, 1989).

» "If I sense a biblical pattern, you would find that the leadership is given to spiritual people who are to decide, to have the oversight of the church, and they lead from the front" (Haddon Robinson, "Power, Preaching & Priorities," *Leadership*, 1:1, Winter, 1980, p. 16).

» "What part of the body is the pastor? Is he not like the cerebellum, the center for communicating messages, coordinating functions, and conducting responses between the head and the body? ...The pastor is not only the *authoritative communicator of the truth* from the Head to the Body, but he is also the *accurate communicator of the needs* from the Body to the Head" (David L. McKenna, "The Ministry's Gordian Knot," *Leadership*, 1:1, Winter, 1980, pp. 50-51).

» "The final responsibility for decisions is that of the company commander [the pastor], and he must answer to the Commander-in-Chief...The Pastor has the power in a growing church.... The pastor of a growing church may appear to outsiders as a dictator, but to the people of the church, his decisions are their decisions" (C. Peter Wagner, *Your Church Can Grow*, Regal, 1987, pp. 66-67).

» "I think the church today is very clergy-dominated. The leadership is clearly clergy leadership, and if one looks closely, one usually finds it is 'specialized' clergy leadership" (Dr. Parker Williamson, "A Look at Laity," *Reformed Theological Seminary Bulletin*, 1995, p. 10).

» "Dinner with the Pastor—Are you new to the church? Come August 18th at 6:30 p.m. on the Tulsa Campus in the Worship Center to check us out."

» "Finding an ordained and experienced minister to lead them was another pressing problem for the frontier congregation. Although the early settlers managed by themselves at first, they were anxious to find a preacher to deliver Sunday services, perform baptisms, officiate at weddings and administer funeral rites. Since full-time ministers were hard to come by, many congregations depended entirely on the services of itinerant preachers who traveled from one community to the next" (Joanna L. Stratton, *Pioneer Women: Voices from the Kansas Frontier*, Simon & Schuster, 1981, p. 179).

» "And we do not have to look at religion in America very deeply before we see that it is saturated with the dogma of the mediator. 'Give us a pastor, give us a priest, give us someone who will do it for us, so that we can avoid intimacy with God ourselves and still reap the benefits'" (Richard J. Foster, *Meditative Prayer*, IVP, 1983, p. 5).

Tragedy of untold proportions lies in the religious superstructure built upon the doctrine of "the pastor," in spite of the fact that *no evidence exists* for this tradition in the documents claimed as the inspired rule of faith and practice—the New Testament (from here on NT). This error in our practice highlights the mistake of putting all our eggs in the basket of "the pastor." Across the board among all Christian groups, denominational and non-denominational, here are the major points of our pastor-doctrine:

> Every church must have a salaried pastor who "sermonizes, marries, buries, baptizes, visits, confronts, counsels, and carries the budget on his back.... He must be a tranquilizer, motivator, stimulator, inspirer and organizer" (James L. Johnson, "The Ministry Can Be Hazardous to Your Health," *Leadership*, 1:1, Winter, 1980, p. 34); if the pastor moves on or dies, a committee must be formed to quickly find a replacement; if a church experiences a split, then the group now "without a pastor" must find one pronto; a new church plant often starts by a pastor moving into a town, renting a storefront, and declaring that he is the " founding pastor" of X-Whatever Church; the sermon is the crescendo of the pastor's duties; the pastor must provide vision and direction for the church; if things go haywire "the pastor is responsible" (Johnson, "Hazardous," p. 34); if attendance or giving drops, the pastor is blamed; the pastor must wear a rack full of hats ("How Many Hats Does Your Pastor Wear?" *Christianity Today*, February 3, 1984, pp. 24-27).

Now I ask you in all candidness—if a new believer, if a person who has been a believer for seven years, if a believer of forty-seven years were to read the NT multiple times—where would they ever find an inkling of all that we have packed into the centrality of "the pastor"? Where is there anything revealed about one person bearing so much responsibility, about one person speaking behind a pulpit or podium, or about, as Puritan John Owen put it, the whole weight of the order, rule, and edification

of the church resting on the pastor? Didn't Paul summarily deny
the possibility of such views by simply stating, *"the Body is not
one part"*?

Assuming you have read the NT, did the pastor-doctrine as
outlined above jump out at you as a vital component of church-
life during your reading? If certain texts came to your mind as
possibly relating to "the pastor," was their specific context taken
into consideration? Do such texts really establish anything pertinent about the dominant presence of the traditional pastor?

How do teachings and practices so foreign to what Jesus said
and did end up being the backbone of visible "Christianity"?
Why is so much staked upon an "office" and its imagined authority when it cannot be justified from any information found in the
NT? Why have gazillions of dollars been invested in seminaries
training students for an occupation that has no basis in Christ's
revealed will? Why have tens of thousands of books been published concerning issues surrounding "the minister" when no
such job description has any Biblical basis?

WHAT IS USED AS EVIDENCE FOR "THE PASTOR"?

Let's ask this question: if the people who teach others to be pastors in seminaries and Bible schools have such brilliant minds,
how can they promote and perpetuate something so off-base
and baseless? Having been involved with this issue since 1965,
here are my observations. First, too many times we justify our
position by reading our way of doing church into NT texts.
Consider, for example, a preacher teaching on 1 Timothy saying, "I can just picture Timothy standing behind a pulpit and
exhorting the people...." Clearly, the image he's evoking takes
elements from modern experience and traditional assumptions
then imposes them on his textual interpretation: (1) that Timothy was a "pastor" and (2) that a pulpit was common church
furniture in the first century. Neither is true, in fact.

Second, *plural* functions actually mentioned in the NT—
elders, overseers, shepherds—too often are just assumed to cor-
respond with the *singular* "office" of "the pastor" and being

applicable to very few. The idea elevating a role to "an office" further implies something special and separate from the common function. The truth is, there is absolutely no connection to how these words are used in the NT with the doctrine of "every church needs one pastor who preaches sermons," etc. (James A. Stahr, "Do Sheep Choose Their Shepherds?" *Interest*, 50:4, April, 1984, p. 2).

Lastly, the most-used common justification I have seen employed to defend the one-pastor system is in suggesting the "messenger" to each of the seven churches in Revelation 2 & 3 was "the pastor." David Fountain believes this when he states,

> In Revelation 2 and 3 the letters to the seven churches are delivered to angels, who are the ministers, and who have a solemn responsibility to the Lord.... In Revelation 1-3 there is a single messenger to whom the message for each church is sent...we must not let our passion for parity blind us to the need of a leader ("Authority & Elders," *The Ideal Church*, Erroll Hulse, ed., 1972, pp. 16, 22).

There is not much in these sentiments to base the entire one-pastor infrastructure system upon. We know for sure that Ephesus, one of the seven churches mentioned in Revelation 2 & 3, had a group of elders, which Paul summoned at one point (*cf.* Acts 20:17). There was no one "minister" in Ephesus. Alexander R. Hay showed the futility of equating an "angel" with "the pastor" when he noted in 1947:

> Seeking something in the NT Church to give ground for the modern position of the Pastor, some have suggested that possibly the "angels" of the seven churches in Asia...occupied such a position. However, there is no true ground for such an interpretation. It is based entirely on supposition. It is opposed to all the other evidence, both Scriptural and historical, which is unanimous in showing that each local church was presided over by several Elders. Surely it is impossible to base, or

to justify, a practice on ground so inadequate (*The New Testament Order for Church & Missionary*, 3rd edition, NTMU, p. 241).

CHURCH IS ALSO BASED ON ONE PERSONALITY

The Passionate Woman

I met an expressive woman the other day
Whose passion blew me away.
Tears filled her eyes as she praised;
By her admiration and love, I sat amazed.
She proclaimed a solid faith and undying trust
With so much love I thought she would combust.
She had a great passion I'd never seen before,
But when she said "my Pastor" I nearly fell on the floor.
The whole time her heart outpoured
I thought she was speaking of Jesus Christ our Lord.

—Kathy Marie Huff

Building the practice of "church" on the *office* of the pastor leads to another monumental aberration: too many churches become dependent on and clustered around the *charismatic personality* of one person, typically their pastor. When Florida senior pastor D. James Kennedy died, it took a very long time to fill his pulpit, then a number of squabbles, disputes and rifts followed when Billy Graham's grandson took over. At the California-based Crystal Cathedral when father Robert Schuller retired, his son was installed. A major disagreement ensued, the son was yanked and Schuller's daughter was put in charge. Then the bills weren't getting paid and the church filed for bankruptcy!

If the 1000 largest churches in America had their primary pastors resign tomorrow, what kind of religious chaos would likely ensue? In all probability, these churches would immediately fall into a tailspin of intense anxiety—not about the spiritual welfare of their broad memberships or their witness to their local communities—but about maintaining attendance, cash flow and their budgets. The absence of that primary, magnetic gift could very well spell the death of such groups as they scramble to secure a comparable *charismatic personality*, with little regard for his/her actual spiritual gifting, provided they fill the enormous void left by the previous charismatic personality.

> "When church members hold to the minister as the one chiefly responsible for the success...or failure of the church," Robert St. Clair notes, "the pastor himself may become party to a conspiracy of hero-worship" (*Neurotics in the Church*, p. 153).

William Enright expressed concern

> "About the power and personality of the charismatic leader, the dynamic preacher. What bothers me—and I have seen it—is that once that person leaves a congregation, the congregation often disintegrates" ("Power, Preaching & Priorities," *Leadership*, 1:1, Winter, 1980, p. 23).

When the pastor "burns out or leaves," David Fitch notes:

> "Half the congregation splits as well, and the people who remain are left holding the bag for the big mortgage the personality left behind."[1]

Why do most folks choose a church? Apparently 90 percent base their choice on the "pastor/preaching."[2] Michael Milton, the Chancellor of Reformed Theological Seminary, notes:

> "Institutions are often held together by the founder or vital leader, who sustains them with the mere power of his personality and gifts" (*Ministry & Leadership*, Winter, 2010, p. 10).

As "clergy," pastors wield a tremendous sway over how churches take shape.

> "Recognize that our congregation sometimes allows us, as ministers, by virtue of our calling, special power and privilege" (L.G. Downing/C.R. Johnson, "How

to Avoid Destructive Behavior," *Ministry*, March 2009,
p. 17).

If we accept that Apostle Paul affirms the obvious—*"the body is not one part,"* then it doesn't take much spiritual discernment to know that "it doesn't make sense to build a church around a personality" (David Fitch, "Sayonara, Senior Pastor") .

Yet that is exactly what the typical pursuit of "church" results in—every aspect of church life hinges on the "success" of the pastor's personality. This system of dependence on one person is a guaranteed crisis-in-the-making since the average pastorate lasts only four to six years!

Why should we be surprised that the visible church is so unhealthy in multiple ways in our times? How would your own body fare if it suddenly became dependent on one part to carry out all its vital functions? You would be in a hospital immediately, if not dead. Yet, we somehow expect life to throb though a church when it is plugged into the performance of one personality. As Einstein noted, *insanity is doing the same thing over and over, and expecting a different result.*

SOME DISASTROUS EFFECTS OF PASTOR-CENTRALITY ON A CHURCH

It should come as no surprise that a system without any NT warrant results in highly counterproductive results.

» Results in *dependency*—A pastor-leader church focus develops the tendency for the people in the pew to be passive, spoon-fed and often totally disoriented without the direction from pastor's pulpit input into their lives.

» Results in *lop-sidedness*—Usually non-spiritual aspects of the pastor's persona, hobbyhorses, personal convictions, weaknesses and habits are reflected in the congregation. Too often this results in the pastor's ideas dominating all body functioning, thereby squelching true and full-member participation. Worse, it removes the pastor from the spiritual correction that can only arise from among equals.

» Results in *sickness in churches*—Pastors frequently complain they cannot get people to help in the church work. Too often, 90 percent of the load is carried by (frequently less than) 10 percent of the membership. Certainly, no everybody-part mentality gets cultivated when the overwhelming feeling among members is, "We're paying the staff to do the visiting, counseling and teaching." Simply put, a body of believers cannot be healthy when the doctrine that the pastor is the "cerebellum"—the center of communication vertically (from God to the body) and horizontally (from the body to God)—is the operating religious assumption.

» Results in *immaturity*—People grow best in open environments where they are respected as persons, where they are encouraged to express themselves, where there are no predetermined boundaries to their functioning, where all are accountable for their actions and where their input is taken seriously. It is very difficult for believers' growth in Christ to prosper within most traditional church structures where the pastor ends up being constantly on center-stage and the primary filter through which all things must be evaluated.

» Results in *abuse*—The inordinate attention given to one part of the body cannot but bring general hurt to the other parts who are thus subordinated. Unfortunately, the traditional pastor-system is also conducive to more specific forms of abuse. Much harm has been brought upon many people by controlling, dominating leaders who cannot tolerate dissent from their vision, or process questions from those under them that challenge the status quo. Rob Bell compares a strong-handed abusive pseudo-parental style to those leaders who use position as a way to dominate others:

> This kind of parent dominates their family with manipulative behavior and petty punishments that create chaos and insecurity for those around them. This kind of parent is using their

strength, but they are actually weak. They do this because in truth, they're broken, confused, and insecure. They have no idea what they're doing, as a parent or a person. The same is true for managers and bosses and teachers and anyone who uses their position of authority to coerce or manipulate or bully others. They can get people to do what they want, but it's only because of the position they hold. Their authority is rooted in nothing larger or stronger or higher than their rank. And that can be taken away tomorrow. They may appear strong, but they are actually weak (Rob Bell, *Sex God*, Zondervan, 2007, pp.102-103; *cf.* Ronald Enroth, *Churches that Abuse*, Zondervan, 1992; Ronald Enroth, *Recovering from Churches that Abuse*, Zondervan, 1994; "Authoritarianism in the Church: The Abuse of Leadership," *Searching Together*, 29:2-3, 2001, 37 pp.).

» Results in the *suppression of others' gifts*—The near-permanent exaltation of one gift necessarily results in the marginalization of many other gifts resident in the body of Christ. Of course, it takes more than one gift to keep a church going, but the clergy-system artifice has the marked tendency to straightjacket the potential that could come to expression through the equally artificial conception of "laity."

» Results in *casualties*—There are many "laypeople" who end up hurt and wounded in the course of pastor-centered church practice; yet, remember that some of the wounded ones *are the pastors themselves*. Bob Moran noted years ago:

A second sociological constant, which surfaces in both Evangelical and Roman Catholic circles is clergy exhaustion (*cf. ML Journal*, 5:2, p. 4).

The [United Methodist] Office of Pastoral Services...finds that clergy burnout continues at a high rate of incidence (*Dimensions*, 20:4, April, 1988, p. 7).

Alan Klaas of Mission Growth Ministries believes about 100,000 parish pastors and their families are currently experiencing career burnout (Hillary Wical, "Clergy Burnout," *Baptists Today*, May, 2001, p. 17).

A 2006 University of Toronto study concluded that Canadian clergy were burned out and isolated (*Christian News*, May 8, 2006, p. 3).

A Seventh-Day Adventist pastor admits that "so many ministers burn out" (Minervino Labrador, Jr., "An Empowering Model for Church Organization," *Ministry*, May, 2010, p. 20).

Is it any wonder that so many clergy fall to the wayside? They are bearing an ecclesiastical load that the Lord never intended anyone to carry *alone*. Imagine what would happen to one part of your physical body if it had to take on the functions of many other body parts. Yet, this is the debilitating position in which adherents to the one-pastor system find themselves.

» Results in *isolation and non-authenticity*—Many pastors become prisoners in their own local churches when they have deep struggles and temptations, but cannot or will not share such things with the perceived "laity." They constantly try to feed others but get no local-body nourishment themselves and so feel compelled to attend "ministers' conferences," attempting to be fed by other clergy. One former Filipino pastor confessed:

> Purity in heart figuratively has more to do
> with honesty and transparency.... Jesus blesses

those who are honest and transparent, for being real before Him and others. But can I? Can I confess my fears and doubts? Can I admit to lust and desire? Can I share my addictions and what possesses me? If I was still in ministry, I could lose my job if I even dare hint to any of those things...to be involved in ministry may mean being dishonest about fears, weaknesses and sins at the pain of losing your livelihood (Bong Manayon, *The Spirituality of Discontentment*, Ekklesia Press, 2011, pp/ 63-64).

A Southern Baptist publication observed:

Ministers are largely dealing with temptation alone...certain theological systems make it difficult for a minister to open up to friends and confidants.... Our independent theology prevents us from being vulnerable. Many ministers feel their congregation has put them on a pedestal and they would let down their flock by admitting temptation.... This notion dangerously isolates ministers (John Hall, "Isolation Leaves Clergy Vulnerable to Sexual Misconduct," *Baptists Today*, January, 2003, p. 33).

Many pastors, therefore, have to find other peer-clergy to talk to. But even this is not easy because, as one church leader admits,

...unfortunately, our sense of position and hierarchy keeps us, sometimes, from finding a ministerial colleague who could serve as a prayer partner (Gerald Klingbeil, "The Gehazi Syndrome," *Ministry*, May, 2010, p. 19).

Further,

...to be frank about the ministry, political, competitive networks overlay much of what is done

in the name of the Lord within the church.
These breed clerical suspicions that form bar-
riers to open communication (J. Grant Swank,
"Who Counsels Ministers When They Have
Problems?" *Christianity Today*, date unknown,
p. 58).

» Results in a *poor representation of Jesus*—Remember that,
first and foremost, the body of Christ is the public representation of Jesus to the world. The pastor-centered (and, to
be fair, the single-elder-centered) body cannot adequately
represent the walk of Jesus to *either* his/her congregation or
within the local community. The task is too disproportionate since we *all* are necessary to Jesus' ultimate testimony
on earth. Make no mistake, though: the world, in the local
community where the body resides, knows what goes on
within the walls and takes note when our behaviors are no
different than those of the "heathen."

"THE BODY IS NOT ONE PART" - A SUMMARY

I am challenging the "church" status quo by highlighting
that there is no NT basis supporting the centrality or necessity of a pastor as the principal functionary within each local
church. I have noted that pastor-dependence is contrary to
Paul's statement that "the body is not one part." This being
true, then it is no wonder that the one-pastor dogma creates
a host of other problems for both churches and those who see
themselves as clergy. We are mortgaging our spiritual future
upon a bankrupt concept.

In light of this, I ask you to carefully read and ponder the following observations made by those who believe in and defend
the one-pastor doctrine. These shocking admissions cannot be
dodged in order to deny that our house is sitting upon some
very rotten timbers. One person gleaned data from several
sources and published sobering information about pastors. He
claims the following:

» 1,500 pastors leave the ministry *each month* in the USA from the unique pressures associated with their job.

» 80 percent of pastors and 84 percent of their spouses feel unqualified and discouraged in their roles.

» 80 percent of seminary and Bible school graduates entering the ministry will leave the ministry within the first five years.

» 70 percent felt God called them to pastoral ministry before their ministry began, but after three years of ministry only 50 percent still felt called.

» 80 percent of pastors surveyed spend less than 15 minutes a day in prayer.

» 70 percent said the only time they spend studying the Word is when they are preparing their sermons.

This report also reveals the feelings of pastors' spouses:

» 80 percent feel their spouse is overworked.

» 80 percent wish their spouse would choose another profession.

» "The majority of pastors' spouses surveyed said that the most destructive event occurring in their marriage and family was the day the pastor entered the ministry."

And never should the feelings of the children of pastors be forgotten:

» "80 percent of adult children of pastors surveyed have had to seek professional help for depression" (The data was collected by Richard A. Murphy; cited by Ivan C. Blake, *cf.* "Pastor for Life," *Ministry*, July/August, 2010, p. 6).

The one particular heart-cry expressed by pastors' wives especially touched and grieved my heart: *"The majority of pastors' spouses surveyed said that the most destructive event that has occurred in their marriage and family was the day the pastor entered the ministry.*" This remark establishes—just from a pragmatic perspective—that there is something very dysfunctional built into the clergy-centrality doctrine. Why would God sacrifice His Bride in such a way? When linked to the fact that there exists no basis for pastor-dependence in the NT, the destructive nature of this system—for all parties involved—is confirmed.

In their book *Pagan Christianity*, Frank Viola and George Barna title chapter five, *"The Pastor: Obstacle to Every-Member Functioning."* They are right. I can think of no tradition that blocks the expression of Christ in his Body more than the *assumption* that every church needs a pastor, lest it fall into disarray.

Jesus himself pointed out that there is only one force, one stronghold that "sets aside" and "nullifies" the revealed will of God—*human traditions* (*cf.* Mark 7:1-23; *cf.*, Frank Viola, *Reimagining Church*, p. 42). It is very possible that the pastor-doctrine stands as one of the most pervasive human traditions causing a log jam in the Christ's expression on the earth through his Bride.

Bob Lewis made this comment, which captures the essence of the deeply rooted disease that infects every part of how church is commonly practiced:

> The truth is, lay people are the heart and core of the church. I challenge every lay person who reads this article to focus on what a tremendous blessing you can be to the kingdom of God, though you may not have a calling to "professional" ministry ("Core Value," *One: The Magazine for Free Will Baptists*, June/July, 2010, p. 12).

There is it again—the division of the Lord's people into "professionals" and "lay people." We must unreservedly jettison this distinction from our hearts and practice the way of Jesus: "you are all brothers and sisters." Otherwise, we are doomed to unending insanity—*doing the same thing over and over again, and expecting a different outcome.*

"THE BODY INDEED IS NOT ONE PART, BUT MANY" (1 COR. 12:14) EKKLESIA: WHERE ALL THE PARTS FUNCTION TOGETHER IN LOVE

> "There is little chance for renewal if all we have is the arrangement by which one speaks and the others listen. One trouble with this conventional system is that the speaker never knows what the unanswered questions are or what reservations remain in the layperson's mentality. Somehow we must arrange opportunities for Christian dialogue since the old idea of the preacher standing ten feet above contradiction simply will not do even for him" (Elton Trueblood, *The Incendiary Fellowship*, 1967).

This traditional way of doing "church" involves a lopsided reliance on one person: the pastor. If it appears that this system seems to "work" outwardly and accomplish many good ends, it is only because we have temporarily masked the deeper problems with invalid testing of what is good. Regardless, the fact remains that the practice itself has no moorings in the NT and ultimately brings with it problems, which cannot remain hidden or ignored.

What I am compelled to ask is: are we interested in the Lord's heart regarding his *ekklesia*?

> There is no medicine without diagnosis. If we pay the high price of trouble in so many churches, we ought to find out what this trouble is saying to us. What is the diagnosis? (Robert J. St. Clair, *Neurotics in the Church*, p. 141).

I suggest that Paul's second letter to the Corinthians (we do not have the first letter, *cf.* 1 Cor. 5:9) highlights the most vital perspectives concerning *organic ekklesia*. The best source elaborating on all these themes is Frank Viola's *Reimagining Church: Pursuing the Dream of Organic Christianity*, and I will unpack the richness of what *ekklesia* means and entails when we come to 1 Corinthians 5, below.

THE EKKLESIA GATHERS AROUND CHRIST ALONE (1 CORINTHIANS 1-4)

Paul spends the opening four chapters of 1 Corinthians dealing with the unhealthy aspect of a *sectarian spirit*. The Corinthians were likely in a situation where those in Apollos' camp were meeting in one home while those of Peter's met in another, etc. There was even a segment that claimed to be "of Christ," which probably met in yet another house.

Part of Paul's response to such foolishness was, "Is Christ divided? Was Paul crucified for you? Or were you baptized in the name of Paul?... But of Him you are in Christ Jesus, who was made to us wisdom from God and righteousness, sanctification and redemption—in order that, as it is written, 'The one boasting, let him boast in the Lord,'" (*cf.* 1 Cor. 1:13, 30, 31).

Brothers and sisters in Christ must function together as they gather around Jesus Christ. This gets tricky because most groups inside and outside of the institutional church claim that Christ is the center of things. But is he? Can Christ be the absolute focus when:

» There are music leaders up front guiding the worship?

» There is such a focus on the pastor, the pulpit and the sermon?

» People come together around unimportant issues, like what Bible version is best, end-times debates and world political issues?

» Traditional church structures dictate what occurs during gatherings instead of the Holy Spirit guiding the parts to express Christ together?

» The group is in reality held together by common experiences, doctrinal systems, or strong personalities?

This is the vital and foremost question each group of believers must face: *Is the life of Christ in us coming to vibrant expression—is Jesus our all in all—in our community life together, in our gatherings together and in our reaching out to the needy?* Anything that stymies, hinders or weakens our expression of Christ should certainly be seriously evaluated.

THE EKKLESIA IS A CARING, SELF-CORRECTING COMMUNITY (1 CORINTHIANS 5)

There was serious immorality in the Corinthian *ekklesia* but they had let it slide. Notice Paul addresses the *entire* believing community as responsible to take action—to gather together as a body. There is no mention of "leaders" having failed in their responsibilities. Even with all their problems, Paul assumes that Christ in their midst by the Holy Spirit will guide them to resolution because the body of Christ *should* care enough to deal with aberrant behavior in its midst in love.

"When you are gathered together" (*cf.* 1 Cor. 5:4) comes to the heart of the meaning and expression of *ekklesia*. Merely translating the word components, many Bible teachers conclude that *ekklesia* means "the called out ones." True enough, but that definition fails to reckon with the *political nature* of this word in the first century. When Jesus announced that he would "build his *ekklesia*," he did not choose a *religious* word like *synagogue*. Instead, he chose the *secular* word *ekklesia*, which would be similar to our concept of a *town meeting*—a place where citizens would get together to take care of matters of common concern in their community. *Ekklesia* was used about 100 times in the Greek translation of the Old Testament to translate the Hebrew word *qahal*, which referred to the Israelite "assembly."

The body of Christ is to be a Spirit-led setting where kingdom business can be acted upon. The *ekklesia* is to be a decision-making, binding/loosing and problem-solving community where Christ is glorified by the proper use of the keys of the kingdom (*cf.* John H. Yoder, "Binding & Loosing," in *The*

Royal Priesthood, Michael G. Cartwright, ed., Eerdmans, 1994, pp. 323-358).

In light of what *ekklesia* really entails, popular conceptions of "church" are dangerously limited to coming to a building, singing, putting some money in a plate, hearing a sermon, and going home. In reality, a loving commitment should flow out of the *ekklesia* that works with others on a wide gamut of kingdom issues. *Ekklesia* is a word that implies *the expression of Christ through the body* in real-time action/reaction to whatever the local community may face.

Contrast this to what most professing Christians in America enjoy as traditional "church," which scarcely intrudes into their normal lifestyle; in fact, it is mostly 'of this world' in both origin and practice. That is why *ekklesia*, which involves a deepening, long-term commitment to others, is barely known in today's world. Traditional church structures have all but completely stifled the *ekklesia* in practice. If the full meaning/practice of *ekklesia* is taken as a starting point, then all that we cherish as "church" must be re-evaluated.

THE EKKLESIA IS A LOVING ENVIRONMENT WHERE DISPUTES CAN BE SETTLED (1 CORINTHIANS 6)

Note that Paul expresses no shock about there being disputes among the believers. What bothered him immensely wasn't that disputes existed but that they were taking each other before unbelieving judges instead of resolving such issues by using the *resources within the ekklesia*. Christ has always intended his *ekklesias* to be loving, forgiving, healing, reconciling, and problem-resolving communities. How utterly different from today's church practices.

Have you ever witnessed or heard of a traditional church that has taken the content of 1 Corinthians 6 seriously? We know that Christians are taking each other to court. We know there are relationship-rupturing disputes taking place. Rumor, defamation, vilification, slander, innuendo and libel abound in what the world sees as common "Christian church" practice. Doesn't the fact that most churches will not touch this hot potato indicate how little we know or are willing to believe about *organic ekklesia*? Helping one another in light of the perspectives of 1 Corinthians 6 is generally not going to happen within the existing church structures that stifle the 58 one another's found throughout the NT.

THE EKKLESIA GATHERS AS BROTHERS & SISTERS TO EXPRESS CHRIST (1 CORINTHIANS 11)

Putting aside the cultural issues (e.g., covering or uncovering of male and female heads), what unfolds here is a picture of a Christian gathering where believers are praying and prophesying together—echoing the emphasis foretold by Joel and proclaimed by Peter on the Day of Pentecost that both sexes would "prophesy" in the Messianic age by the Spirit's leading (*cf*. Acts 2:16-18). On that day, before Peter opened his mouth to proclaim Jesus, 120 men and women had just spoken the wonderful works of God in foreign languages. Regarding Paul's statement, "when any woman prays or prophesies," (*cf*. 1 Cor. 11:5) C.K. Barrett noted:

> The verse is meaningless unless women were from time to time moved, in the Christian assembly in Corinth, to pray and prophesy aloud in public.... If moreover Paul had thought it wrong for them to do this he would certainly not have wasted time in discussing what...they should do with their heads; he would simply have forbidden the practice (*cf. The First Epistle to the Corinthians*, Harper & Row, 1968, p.250; *cf*. p. 331).

THE EKKLESIA IS CHRIST'S BODY ON EARTH: ALL THE PARTS ARE VITAL (1 CORINTHIANS 12)

As Christ comes to expression through his people, Paul makes several things crystal clear. First, in 1 Corinthians 12:7, we see that each and every believer is given at least one manifestation of the Spirit *profiting the rest of the body*. The phrase "manifestation of the Spirit" involves much more than mere housekeeping. As David Prior notes,

> the most important truth here stressed is that individual Christians are intended to *demonstrate* that they have the Spirit of God within them.... [The Spirit] intends to make himself felt and known through his gifts, as well as by his fruit (*The Message of 1 Corinthians*, IVP, 1985, p. 197).

Second, in 1 Corinthians 12:14 —as I have previously stressed—no body (physical or spiritual) can be healthy when it depends on one office or personality or any other single aspect. Health is always linked to the interdependent functioning and contribution of *all* the diverse parts. Pastors admit the reality that most church work is done by a very small percentage of the "members," which should be a red flag warning that something is way out of kilter. In fact, too often, the church structures in place prohibit the life of Christ coming to *any* expression through each and every part.

> Many Christians do not, or cannot, manifest their distinctive gifts in the life of their local church (*cf.* David Prior, *1 Corinthians*, p. 198).

This clearly supports the importance of having *an atmosphere of acceptance, openness and freedom—a setting where Jesus is welcome to accomplish his purposes—a setting where there is no "clergy/ laity" division—a setting where brothers and sisters can express the Lord together in love.*

Third, Paul turns everything upside-down by suggesting the opposite of where we have since traditionally put the emphasis. We are seriously infected with a celebrity mentality where the gift of gab reigns—as if the whole body is dependent on a "mouth"! But Paul in 1 Corinthians 12:22-24, teaches that "the parts that seem to be weaker are necessary, and the ones we think to be less honorable should have more abundant honor bestowed on them." Paul's perspectives seem foreign and out of place considering how church was and is practiced from 1500 years ago even to today. *Ekklesia* is a context where all the Lord's people are respected and honored.

THE EKKLESIA GATHERS IN OPENNESS AROUND JESUS CHRIST (1 CORINTHIANS 14)

Here we get the clearest NT glimpse of first century *ekklesia* meetings. The only reason we have this peek into the Corinthian situation is because there were problems going on. Paul's correction does not consist of shutting down their open meeting. Instead, he gives them perspectives to guide their times together—a crucial one being, "let all things be done for the building up of one another."

A lingering question I wrestled with for years is: Why does this revelation about a Christian gathering in 1 Corinthians 14 get essentially tossed out the window as irrelevant in favor of a more structured "worship service," which typically focuses on the pastor and his/her sermon? My suggestion is that we are missing tremendous blessings in Christ by being blind and deaf to the implications of this passage for our practice of church. There are several key points that emerge from 1 Corinthians 14 and its context.

First, *the believers gathered together around Jesus Christ* (*cf.* 1 Cor. 11:23-26; 1 Cor. 10:16-17, 21). In Acts 20:7, we are told that the *ekklesia* came together for the purpose of breaking bread. They ate together and remembered the Lord (1 Cor. 11:33; *cf.*, "The Lord's Supper in the Life of the Church," *Searching Together*, 12:3, Autumn, 1983, 32 pp.). *There is no other reason for the ekklesia to gather except the living Christ.* The body comes together as the expression—to and through one another—of what the Lord Jesus has done in history and in their lives.

Next, *this was an open gathering, which welcomed Jesus to meet with them and glorify himself by the Spirit's leading.* There was no group or single "up front" leaders conducting the meeting. What happened during the gathering was not pre-determined, but was always open to the Spirit's guidance in showing things concerning Christ. However, it would be incorrect to assume nothing was ever planned ahead of time by the mutual consent of the body—but such plans were always subject to the Spirit leading in a different direction.

Third, *this was a body meeting in which all participated according to the Spirit's leading.* One person might sing a song that the Lord had given them; perhaps the group might sing this song too. Another might have a teaching to set before the brothers and sisters, accompanied with questions and discussion. Someone might pose a question to the group that has been troubling them. Others may have burdens and concerns that need prayer.

An open meeting does not mean that everybody present *has* to say something; it doesn't mean that *anyone* has to say something *always.* It does mean that there is an atmosphere where anything needing to be said *can* be spoken by anyone. Alexander McClaren commented on the flavor of what was taking place in 1 Corinthians 14:

> Everyone of us has something, and no one of us has everything (*Expositions of Holy Scripture: Romans/Corinthians,* Hartford, CT: S.S. Scranton Co., CA. 1905, p. 184).

I am amazed that there is nearly always somebody, somewhere who manifests great light in a dark context. Ponder these astute insights from David Thomas' comments on 1 Corinthians 14 in *1898!*

> The Christian church in assembly, on the same occasion, might have several speakers to address them.... If this be so: 1. Should Christian teaching be regarded as a *profession?* It is so now: persons are brought up in it, trained for it, and live by it, as architects, lawyers, doctors.... 2. Is the Christian church justified in confining its attention to the *ministry of one person?* In most modern congregations there are some Christian people who by natural ability, by experimental knowledge and inspiration, are far more qualified to instruct and con-

front the people than their professional and stated minister. Surely official preaching has no authority, either
in Scripture, reason, or experience, and it must come
to an end sooner or later. Every Christian should be a
preacher. Were the half-hour allotted in church services
for the sermon to be occupied by three or four Christ-
like persons...with the capability of expression withal,
it would not only be far more interesting, but more
profitably spent than now (*The Pulpit Commentary:
1 Corinthians*, F.W. Farrar & David Thomas, Funk &
Wagnalls, 1898, pp. 429-433).

Why do we throw out the revelation of 1 Corinthians 14 and
make the typical service found in church bulletins so unchal-
lengeable and sacrosanct? How do church leaders respond when
it is suggested that it might be better to have an open, participatory meeting where believers could exalt Christ with their contributions? Often they admit that the early church was informal
and open, but then they give reasons and excuses why we can't
do that kind of thing now, and that multiple participation must
take place in settings outside the main church-gathering.

Here are two such examples. Leonard Coppes (Orthodox
Presbyterian) creatively dodges 1 Corinthians 14 by saying:

In Paul's day the worship service probably was more
open than are today's services... This would not be
wrong were we to do this today as long as the entire
congregation would be willing to stay at worship until the sermon and questions were brought to a proper
conclusion. In NT times several hours were normally
spent in worship (*cf.* Acts 20:7-9). In modern times we
tend to compress the service into about an hour's time.
Consequently, we follow the *preaching* system without
public questions in order to make our time most profitable. Questions are asked at the door of the church,
over the phone, or by other private interviews (*Are Five*

Points Enough? The Ten Points of Calvinism, 1980, pp. 182-183).

Coppes' analysis fails on several fronts. First, where is it written that all questions must be brought "to their proper conclusion" within either the context of a sermon or, for that matter, any teaching? It can take extensive time to think through and consider difficult teachings adequately. Second, his worship conception derives from the already demonstrated flawed model instituted hundreds of years *after* the time covered by Paul's Corinthian epistle; he imputes his modern practice backwards into a historical context. Finally, his argument is fallacious because it assumes—without proof—that the modern model cited is "profitable." He basically then completely denies that there is any benefit at all to others hearing questions and answers because his emphasis lies upon "private interviews." Taken together, he's clearly unwilling to practice what he knows is in 1 Corinthians 14, so he just pushes it aside in order to perpetuate the tradition of pulpit-centrality.

Herbert Carson was a Calvinistic Baptist pastor in England who admitted that:

> ...the glimpses we have of worshipping congregations in the New Testament are of active participants.

But in order to maintain preaching as the center-point, he suggests that churches must have "smaller gatherings" outside of the big meeting

> ...if this vital New Testament element of participation is to be preserved (*Hallelujah! Christian Worship,* 1980, pp. 29, 31).

You might think that if Carson and Coppes saw something revealed in the NT, they would pursue it. In the case of 1 Corinthians 14, however, they discount the instructive information they admit is there in order to continue sermon-centered, non-participatory traditional meetings.

1 Corinthians 11:17-20 and 1 Corinthians 14 have the *main gathering* of the saints in view—"coming together in *ekklesia*"—"if therefore the whole *ekklesia* comes together." So, why don't we "come together" like the early church did? Why do we adhere to a bulletin-guided, pastor-led traditional church service while rejecting an uplifting, Christ-centered, Spirit-led, open and participatory gathering? Why do we omit, ignore, dismiss or skip over this NT teaching?

A great deal of reluctance to enter into a new way of being *ekklesia* has to do with *fear*. It's new. It's different. It isn't what most people have experienced as church meetings with leaders up front. They have never seen the practice of simplicity in Christ as it came to expression in the first century. People are almost always afraid of change.

We are afraid of doing church without a human leader. Except, the truth is, we do have a Leader—*Jesus Christ*. Further, the practical reality is that every group will have leadership each time they get together. His Spirit always leads the saints to express Christ one to another in a diverse ways; not in a traditional, concrete *pro forma* format. One sister may share something that becomes the theme that others build on—in one meeting or in several; for a day or for months, even years of interaction. Another time, a brother may tell how the Lord ministered to him in the past week, and that leads to different things, which go on from there. The point is, in organic meetings *His Spirit leadership is gracious, fluid and over a period of time involves everyone.* If a group looks to the same person time after time to get and to keep things rolling by solely providing the essential content of the gathering, then *the living Christ blossoming through all the parts* is soured.

Sadly, in this way I am convinced that we are all like Israel—*we want a visible king.* Read 1 Samuel 8 and see how Israel was not satisfied with having *the invisible God* as their Leader; they wanted to be *like the nations around them* who had visible human kings. It underscores human desire of having someone else tell us what vision to follow, where to meet, what to do, and what to believe—in short, to spoon-feed us like children—thus, we *reject the Lord's leadership,* substituting a vastly inferior system in his place.

We all will have a king. The crucial question is, will our king be *visible* or *Invisible?* Will we run church like the corporations in the world—in other words, be like the world—or will seek higher satisfaction in *following the One, whom having not seen, we love?*

Do not be mistaken! These behaviors are not limited to the traditional "church" experience. I have seen this phenomenon kill the life expression in simple gatherings just as frequently. It is the existence of pastor-wannabe's, elder-wannabe's and former church officials who come to such a group claiming a false non-scriptural basis to "improve" their gatherings. Even among those who have completely left the institutional church, too often there is tendency to look for former "leaders" in past settings to provide the impetus for what takes place in the new one.

Those from leadership positions in the institutional church must take their ambitions and history of being "up front" to the cross. They must take their proper place as just another brother or just a sister amongst other brothers and sisters. If not, the group will inevitably revert to an institutional form usurping Jesus' leadership. Simply meeting in a home does not, in any way, ensure that a Christian group functions under Jesus' Lordship. The pressing issue here is whether or not a person or group takes the place of Christ at the center of any fellowship meeting.

We are afraid of trusting the Lord with unknowns. Fear is a natural partner to confronting the unknown. For the believer, however, fear is the outcome of not trusting in Jesus Christ. His perfect love casts out fear. People focus on a human king because they do not trust the King. To come together as believers and not have a bulletin that lists everything that will happen between 11 a.m. and 12 p.m. Sunday morning is rather uncomfortable for most people. Gathering as saints and trust Jesus by his Spirit to guide every aspect of their time together is truly a wonderful and blessed experience. To come together in a room with other redeemed people and not know exactly what will take place goes against the worldly method of controlling your environment to conquer fear. Every grain of the "natural man" yearns *for a leader to keep us safe within the religious box.* But we *do* have a Leader. We must have faith allowing for Him to glorify himself through us without the box.

We are afraid to be vulnerable. Truth be told, everything in organic church *grows out of deepening relationships in Christ.* Thus, you cannot have an enriching 1 Corinthians 14 meeting without those attending getting to know each other during the normal course of life apart from the meetings. This, too, challenges us to live other than those "of this world" with a willingness to pursue long-term, deep relationship-building, which only comes from being vulnerable to the observations and interactions of others who are also in Christ (*cf.* Bill Thrall/Bruce McNicol/John S. Lynch, *TrueFaced: Trusting God & Others with Who We Really Are*, NavPress, 2004, 160 pp.).

Such vulnerability in the presence of the brothers and sisters only takes place when we feel comfortable in a loving, accepting atmosphere filled with the aroma of Jesus. What a huge chasm between a 1 Corinthians 14 gathering and a regular church service. You can work your way through the elements in a church bulletin with no commitment or love whatsoever to anyone in the pews around you. On the other hand, built in to the lively, engaging meeting of the *ekklesia*—where all are participating— is a Christ-focused caring and interest in others. An open meeting where Jesus is actively being lifted up through many voices is probably not going to feel comfortable to anyone used to being emotionally-disengaged and passively listening to weekly sermons.

We are afraid of silence. This deserves reinforcement: we don't handle silence well at all. In our culture and in church buildings we are used to hearing sounds—media, music, human talking. We are, in fact, far too used to entertainment keeping us from thinking about the thoughts in our own heads. As a result, many people get downright agitated during any season of silence. In an open, organic 1 Corinthians 14 meeting there is nothing wrong with periods, short or long, of silence. Quietness is very healthy: "Be still, and know that I am God." Most of us have, at one time or another, experienced moments when the things of Christ were so overwhelming that the only appropriate response was silent awe.

Can things go wrong in an open meeting? Are there problems connected to Christ-centered open gatherings? Of course! But not because something is wrong with Paul's model but because where ever people interact, "problems" will arise. This is not only good but also necessary. We cannot grow if we do not bump into things, which cause us to think and go back to the Fountain of God's Spirit in Jesus. The Corinthians had issues which Paul addressed. Some talked too much; some seemed sealed in silence. Essentially, though, Paul answers, however simplistic sounding, with the truth that *if the saints are captured by the love of Christ, if they are resting in him as their all and all, if they are pursuing him every day, and if the love of God is being poured into their hearts by the Holy Spirit—when people like this come together to share Jesus with one another, a lot of the kinks and rough edges will melt away into insignificance.* When believers are madly in love with Jesus, a lot of imperfections in others can be easily covered!

CONCLUDING THOUGHTS

The same *Ministry* magazine that started off by advocating, "the local church pastor is key—absolutely central—to everything we are and do as a church," ended with a book review of a commentary on 1 and 2 Timothy/Titus by a Roman Catholic author. The reviewer noted this pertinent information:

> The historical and archaeological background is also put to effective use, as in his observation that "Christians did not build churches until after the Edict of Toleration in 313 C.E." and that earlier Christian assemblies were held in private homes that were only later enlarged

and remodeled such as Peter's house in Capernaum and the house church in Dura Europos (Clinton Wahlen, "Resources," *Ministry*, July/August, 2010, p. 60).

Source after source recognizes the early church was simple. It had no pastor-system, no buildings and no tax benefits. Yet this was a time of unparalleled spiritual growth and spread of the gospel. It would seem that many people in our day are now interested in taking their cues from the NT instead of ancient traditions and contemporary marketing techniques.

Francis Chan in his popular book, *Crazy Love*, expresses some great-sounding thoughts with passion, but in reality a serious problem looms beneath them:

> I'm a pastor first and foremost, and I'm trying to offer a solution or a model of what church should look like. I'm going back to Scripture and seeing what the church was in its simplest form and trying to re-create that in my own church. I'm not coming up with anything new. I'm calling people to go back to the way it was (p. 180).

The far-reaching problem is this: *if the church is looked at the way it was in its simplest form as portrayed in the NT, nothing can be found about anyone being "a pastor first and foremost"!* The truth is, *the traditional doctrine of "the pastor" has no clothes!*

I think the best words to end this essay with are ones I wrote thirty years ago in 1981:

> Some might feel that churches are not "ready" for the truths that have been discussed in this article. But why should *truth* be postponed? Were churches "ready" to practice the responsibilities of priesthood a hundred years ago? Fifty? Twenty? If years of tradition are wrong, just when will we be "ready" to edify one another, as we should? If something important is missing in our churches, then the time has come for us to implement what Christ has revealed. The implications of a functioning priesthood probably seem "radical" only be-

cause we are used to patterns of tradition, which have no foundation in Scripture.

We must ask ourselves if our churches are being prepared for future suffering. Our current "freedoms" with reference to assembling together may be disrupted some day by governmental upheaval. Are the saints being prepared *now* to care and sacrifice for one another? What if all evangelical pastors were arrested? Would the churches be in a position to continue functioning? The possibility of an underground church in the future—which is a *reality* in many places—should cause us to reflect upon our preparedness for such a situation. Learning to care and minister to one another now is an essential ("Building Up the Body: One Man or One Another?").

The church traditions built around one "office" and the personality that occupies the pulpit is a monumentally disproportionate aberration. This model portrays the idea that the body of Christ depends on *one part*. Unless and until we cast out this demon-like paradigm once and for all, we will just continue to suppress the full expression of Christ, which comes only through the *many parts*.

ENDNOTES:

1. www.outofur.com/archives/2007/02/sayonara_senior.html

2. http://churchrelevance.com/
   qa-top-reasons-for-church-attendance

ROMANCING THE PASTORATE

A RESPONSE TO EUGENE PETERSON'S *THE PASTOR: A MEMOIR*
(HARPERONE, 2011, 320PP.)

We would expect a well-written book from Eugene Peterson, and it is a great read. It chronicles the author's life as a pastor, and highlights the various experiences he had as time elapsed that enhanced his growth as a church leader. This is a *memoir*— Eugene is assuming, not trying to establish, the propriety and necessity of "the pastor" as a starting point, and then unfolds his life as it fits into this long-standing tradition. His personal narrative provides an opportune springboard to reflect on life's revelations, and to critique the institution of "the pastor."

MONTANA

Peterson speaks fondly of his upbringing in rural Montana.

> This place has provided a protected space and time to become who I am. It has been a centering and deepening place of prayer and meditation, reflection and understanding, conversation and reading (p.11).

I identify with these sentiments, for I spent most of my summers, from the ages of ten to eighteen, on the northwest Kansas farm of my mother's parents. My most cherished childhood memories are rooted in my wanderings on the land, and the experiences of the sounds, the smells, the people, the animals, and the sunsets found in Smith County, Kansas. The water was drawn from a pump on the front porch, and the calls of nature were answered in an outhouse. Life here added valuable dimensions to the life of a young man used to the city-life around Los Angeles, California!

HIS MOTHER PREACHED

Eugene recalls how his mother's preaching and storytelling helped forge his imagination when, from the age of three to six,

this then twenty-three year old woman took him as her chaper-
one to Sunday night meetings in various locations. Rough log-
gers and miners came to sing, hear her proclaim biblical stories,
and have her pray for them. These men—never a woman in the
audience—would openly weep, "honking into their red bandan-
nas, wiping their tears without embarrassment" (p.28).

When Eugene was six, the meetings stopped because his sister was born.

> I heard the best preaching of my lifetime those nights—
> and the most colorful cursing.... Later, when I was a
> teenager, I asked her why she never started up the Sun-
> day night meetings again. She told me that a man, hav-
> ing learned of what she was doing, confronted her after
> Sunday-morning worship in our church with an open
> Bible and read to her: "Let a woman learn in silence
> with all submissiveness. I permit no woman to teach
> or to have authority over men; she is to keep silent."
> She kept silent.... by the time she was intimidated into
> silence, she had achieved something formative and last-
> ing in me, an artesian spring of song and story (p.33).

Here, again, poor translation from Greek to English lays
waste to heart-felt service; the Greek word used in 1 Timothy
2 is *heseuchia*, which does not mean "silence" but "quietness."
The same word is used in 1 Timothy 2:2 where Paul suggests
that goal for all believers is to lead a "quiet" life. In *What's
With Paul & Women? Unlocking the Cultural Background to 1
Timothy 2*, I develop a more accurate interpretation of 1 Timothy
2:9-15, showing how the Paul's purpose here is not to silence
female participation.

THE AMERICAN BRAND OF RELIGION

Throughout the book Peterson displays a marked disdain, to his
credit, for the "American way" in religion, which caters to "ram-
pant consumerism that treats God as a product to be marketed"
(p.4). He saw how the church was viewed as "an ecclesiastical

business with a mission to market spirituality to consumers and make them happy" and as "a business opportunity that would cater to the consumer tastes" (p.111). "Entertainment, cheerleading, and manipulation were conspicuous in high places.... Programs had developed into the dominant methodology of 'doing church'" (p.254).

NOT A PRETTY PICTURE

There can be little doubt that Eugene's Montana up bringing did not inspire much respect for pastors. The ones ministering in the sectarian church his family attended "seemed marginal to the actual business of living," and "outside of the morning our family spent with them each Sunday, none—there was one significant exception—seemed particularly interested in God" (p.3). Along these same lines, throughout the book Peterson notes concerning problems at work in the traditional pastorate:

» "Men and women who are pastors in America today find that they have entered into a way of life that is in ruins" (p.4).

» "Many pastors, disappointed or disillusioned with their congregations, defect after a few years and find more congenial work.... In the fifty years that I have lived the vocation of pastor, these defections and dismissals have reached epidemic proportions in every branch and form of church" (p.5).

» "I couldn't see that God or place—holy God, sacred place— was a significant consideration in forming a pastoral identity in America" (p.13)

» "As I entered adolescence, I began to get the feeling that God, except for the time they talked about him on Sunday, was not high on their agenda. They were pretty full of themselves" (p.71).

» "Tim said, 'Eugene, did you see us talking, the way *she* was talking—that intensity? I wish I could do that kind of thing all day, every day. Every time I come in here and there are no customers, she wants to talk about prayer and her life.' 'So why don't you do it—have conversations like that?' 'Because I have to run this damn church'.... Why did he find the diner a more hospitable venue for being a pastor than the church?" (p.145).

» Pastors "were lonely, and sometimes angry that they were lonely" (p.149).

» "We were seeing pastors left and right abandoning their vocations and taking jobs" (p.165).

» "We talked together about the dangers of being a pastor in America, where the magnificent church, like the magnificent Rocky Mountains, 'has twenty different ways to kill you'" (p.211).

» "I didn't want to be a pastor in the ways that were most in evidence and most rewarded in the American consumerist and celebrity culture" (p.242).

» "One evening after dinner, Karen—she was five years old at the time—asked me to read her a story. I said, 'I'm sorry, Karen, but I have a meeting tonight.' 'This is the twenty-seventh night in a row you have had a meeting.' She had been keeping track, counting" (p.225).

"THE PASTOR"

While Peterson freely confesses the numerous concerns connected to being a pastor, he nevertheless has sought to structure and live out his life with the pastoral vocation as his template. For him, everything of importance boils down to "pastor and congregation"—more accurately, "pastor/pastor's wife and congregation" (pp.28-29, 114, 116, 151). Eugene sees himself in the flow of "our two-thousand-year pastoral tradition" (p.5).

Certainly, this ever-present practice has taken various shapes over the course of post-apostolic history. But it must be asked; *can the assumption that every local church must have an ordained pastor be validated in the NT?* Repeatedly in the book Peterson expresses a desire to walk in a biblically informed manner—"I wanted my life, both my personal and working life, to be shaped by God and the Scriptures and prayer," (p.5; *cf.* pp. 3, 6, 21, 107, 151, 183, 227, 286).

However, in the pages of the NT there is absolutely nothing about the centrality and indispensability of "the pastor" who occupies a vocation, which fulfills the following activities described by Peterson:

» "Who else in the community other than the pastor has the assigned task of greeting men and women and welcoming them into a congregation...?" (p.137).

» "The only way the Christian life is brought to maturity is through intimacy, renunciation, and personal deepening. And the pastor is in a key position to nurture such maturity" (p.157).

» "I had a role that was recognizable as pastor: I led worship and preached on Sunday, I visited the sick and distraught, I administered the affairs of the congregation, I prayed with and for people" (p.189).

» "I had initiated the prayers on the congregation's Sunday Sabbath" (p.221).

» "These men and women, I think without exception, know the difference between dealing with alcoholism as a problem, which they are doing in their recovery, and living a life of faith in Christ as a gift and accepting me as their pastor as they do it" (p.263). "In a few months she became a Christian and I became her pastor" (p.271).

» "Every Sunday after a morning of leading my congregation in worship, I walked the quarter of a mile home" (p.273).

» "There is a long tradition in the church's life that the pastoral vocation consists in preparing people for a 'good death'" (p.289).

How, then, could this vocational agenda be discovered from reading the NT? The only specific biblical allusion Eugene offers in the book for "the pastor" is a real stretch.

> A few weeks into teaching the course [on Revelation], I began imagining myself with John of Patmos as a pastor. John, doing his work on the prison island of Patmos, was exiled from the seven congregations that he served as a pastor.... I realized that John's vocation as pastor was not confined to those seven sermons addressed to his miniscule congregations, but got expressed in the urgency and sovereignty and beauty and drama that pervaded the entire book.... Pastor John of Patmos provided the biblical DNA that gave me my identity as pastor" (pp.19-20, 237).

This imaginative reasoning is slim pickings upon which to build the entire superstructure of "the pastor" doctrine! There is no explicit evidence that John was "the pastor" of the seven congregations mentioned in Revelation 2 & 3. It is yet another case where Peterson, like so many others, "reads" modern practice *into* the NT text by suggesting Christ's words to these seven churches were "sermons" by John.

Peterson's pillar comes tumbling down when we recall that in Acts 20 Paul called for the "elders" (plural) of the *ekklesia* (singular) in Ephesus—the first city addressed in Revelation 2:1-7. Clearly, the Ephesian church had no one person functioning as "the pastor." "The pastor" as defined by Eugene in his book simply is not to be found in the NT documents. Yet visible Christianity has become anchored to the concept and physical presence of clergy or "the pastor." We must re-visit the foundations of church practice as we know it.

CLERGY/LAITY

Peterson purports that "one of the achievements of the Protestant Reformation was a leveling of the ground between clergy and laity" (p.280). This is a historically inept assumption and a most misleading statement at several levels. First, the Protestant Reformers all strongly insisted upon and advocated for the division between clergy and laity; they just wanted Protestant clergy to be in charge instead of the former Roman Catholic leadership. They wanted their own pulpit to be the center point instead of the sacramental altar table.

Secondly, in theory the Protestant conception of the "priesthood of all believers" was essentially *individualistic* wherein a believer had direct access to Christ and the scriptures with no need for human mediators. In practice, this was almost always enormously diluted by the insistence upon their own preeminent 'pastoral' leadership, which, in turn, meant they could not develop the *corporate* dimension of the priesthood because of the inordinate attention given to the clergy, and the distinction between the ordained and non-ordained. In the NT, the terms "clergy" (Greek: *kleros*) and "laity" (Greek: *laos*) both apply to the same group—*all of God's people without distinctions.*

CHRIST IN ALL THE SCRIPTURES

Eugene makes some great points regarding *how* the Bible is approached and handled. As a lad growing up he admits that he was not "fond of it," and was actually "bored with it" (p.84).

> More often than not it was a field of contention, providing material for truths that were contested by warring factions. Or it was reduced to rules and principles that promised to keep me out of moral potholes. Or, and this was the worst of all, it was flattened into clichés and slogans and sentimental god talk intended to

inspire and motivate.... Until now, I and all the people
I associated with had treated the Bible as something
to be *used*—used as a textbook with information about
God, used as a handbook to lead people to salvation,
used as a weapon to defeat the devil and all his angels,
used as an antidepressant (pp.84-85).

First and foremost, the Scriptures are about the living Word
of God, Jesus Christ—"Moses wrote about me." As Isaac
Watts penned, "But in Your written Word/ The volumes of
my Father's grace/ Does all my griefs assuage/ Here I behold
my Savior's face in every page." "Therefore," Martin Luther
asserted, "he who would correctly and profitably read Scripture
should see to it that he finds Christ in it."

THE EARLY CHURCH

Peterson acknowledges that "the first three centuries of Christian churches were cave churches—unobtrusive house churches
and catacombs" (p.170). It seems this fact's significance is usually glossed over as if it stands as an irrelevant footnote for us. I
would like to suggest that a pattern of Christ-centered simplicity unfolds in the NT. Jesus desires for himself to be expressed
through his body in this age (*cf.* Eph. 3:10). Eugene notes that
"all the great realities that we can't touch or see take form on
ground that we *can* touch and see" (p.12). I agree, which means
that—to a watching world—the invisible heavenly realities on
earth can only be seen *in the properly functioning body of Christ*—
where *all* parts work together, not just a select few paid staff.

Peterson rightly points out that "the *way* we learn something
is more influential than the something we learn. No content
comes into our lives free-floating: it is always embedded in a
form of some kind" (p. 33). It would seem that the primary
way we grow in Christ's body is through communicating Christ
with one another in an open atmosphere. It is universally agreed
by communication experts that a *monologue* is the worst possible way to learn. Even Eugene concedes, "we don't grow and

mature in our Christian life by sitting in a classroom and library...
or by going to church and singing and listening to sermons" (p.
230). Yet the sermon form yields the practical result of shutting
down the open "every-part" participation vital to our growth
and to our witness (*cf.* John H. Yoder, "The Rule of Paul," *Body
Politics*, Herald Press, 1992, pp. 61-70).

THE PASTOR NOT NOTICED?

Eugene suggests this goal: "You are at your pastoral best when
you are not noticed. To keep this vocation healthy requires constant self-negation, getting out of the way" (p.292). If this is
truly carried to its logical conclusion, then the pastoral system
is unfortunately dysfunctional, since it is designed to cultivate
and foster attention and dependence on one part: "the pastor." Which is why it is almost impossible to keep this vocation healthy for any meaningful length of time—it requires one
person to bear the brunt of church vision, growth, and health,
which is an impossibility. The nature of the beast makes sure one
person is either a hero or a scapegoat. Neither seems to reflect
Jesus' will for his bride.

A MARGINAL MINORITY

A most profound insight arrives from Peterson in his persuasion
that *smallness* not largeness will be most effective in forwarding
Christ's kingdom.

> [I came to] a developing conviction that the most effec-
> tive strategy for change, for revolution—at least on the
> large scale that the Kingdom of God involves—comes
> from a minority working from the margins...that a mi-
> nority people working from the margins has the best
> chance of being a community capable of penetrating
> the non-community, the mob, the depersonalized,
> function-defined crowd that is the sociological norm of
> America (p.16).

It is my heart-felt conviction that this *marginal minority* will penetrate our alienated, wounded, impersonal culture best with forms outside of the institutional church. The traditional pastor-centered form is just not going to cut it—from a biblical or pragmatic perspective. As Eugene asked after his pastor friend was frustrated about being pulled from real service to people "because I have to run this damn church"—*Why did he find the diner a more hospitable venue for being a pastor than the church?*

— **Jon Zens**
April, 2011

BUILDING UP THE BODY:

ONE MAN OR ONE-ANOTHER?

(This article scrutinizes the Reformed/Puritan view of the ministry, and seeks to understand and underscore the priesthood of all believers. It originally appeared in Baptist Reformation Review, *10:2, Summer, 1981)*

I have many things on my heart that I would like to share with you concerning the building-up of the church. In "The Local Church: The Pillar and Ground of the Truth" (*Baptist Reformation Review*, Summer, 1977), I set forth some broad principles regarding the importance of the local church in the believer's life. There I said, in commenting on Hebrews 10:24-25, "these verses involve much more than just sitting thirty to sixty minutes before the preached Word.... Something more is to happen when we assemble with the brethren...preaching only is not enough." Further consideration of these matters, however, has led me to believe that there are some problems in our general outlook and practice, which simply militate against this "something more" being expressed. In what follows, I wish to explore some Scriptural and historical matters, which bear on the manner in which the body of Christ is to be built up. Traditionally and practically we have ended up focusing on one person, the "pastor"; I submit that the NT focuses on "one another" in the building-up process.

If we are serious about Christ's truth, then we should not be afraid to bring our private and local church practices under the scrutiny of God's Word. John Owen made the following observation in 1689:

> For the most part, the churches that are in the world at present know not *how they came so to be*, continuing only in that state, which they have received by tradition from their fathers (*The True Nature of a Gospel*

Church, edited and abridged by John Huxtable [London, 1947], p. 35).

There are things in our tradition that are in conflict with the NT revelation. We need to correct our practice. I have attempted to speak in areas where clearness, not haziness, is evident in the NT. The questions I raise and the convictions I state may seem to be strong; but I ask you to consider these things in the light of Scripture, and if you believe there is Scriptural teaching I have missed, or perverted, please seek to correct me. I believe these matters are of utmost importance, and it is critical that we ascertain the mind of Christ concerning the place of mutual ministry in the local church. According to Ephesians 4:16, we need that which *every joint supplies* in order to grow in Christ.

THE NEW TESTAMENT PERSPECTIVE: THE PRIORITY OF THE BODY

The Broad Vantage Point:
A Functioning Priesthood 1 Peter 2:5,9

Just as there was a people of God in the old age, so now under the New Covenant there is an "Israel of God" (*cf.* Gal. 6:16). But this new people is not *national*, but *spiritual* in character— "living stones." That which was typified in geographical Israel has now come to living expression in "a spiritual house, a holy priesthood," which "offers up spiritual sacrifices" (v. 5). This house is built upon the foundation of Jesus Christ (v. 4; *cf.* 1 Cor. 3:11).

Of special interest to us here is the conception of this family of God as "a holy priesthood...a royal priesthood" (vv. 5, 9). Jesus fulfilled the Old Covenant priesthood, and is building a church in which every "living stone" is a "priest." There were many requirements for the Old Covenant priesthood, and as a result only a relatively few males functioned in it. But the New Covenant priesthood includes all saints—all believing men, women and children.

More importantly, however, is the fact that the Old Covenant priests had *certain functions* to constantly perform. Peter focuses on this point: New Covenant priests *function* by offering up "spiritual sacrifices" (v. 5). A non-functioning priesthood is an absurdity! What is included in "spiritual sacrifices" can be seen clearly in such passages as Romans 12:1-8 (*cf.* Heb. 13:15-16; Rev. 5:8).

In Romans 12:1-8, it is important to see how Paul naturally links our priesthood (v. 1) with our functioning in the body: "so we, being many, are one body in Christ, and every one members one of another. Having then gifts differing according to the grace that is given to us" (vv. 5-6). Not "all members have the same function" (v. 4), but *all members are to function in the body* (v. 3b). It should also be clear that the functions Paul has in view involve (though not exclusively) the meetings where the church comes together (vv. 6-8). There are four things with reference to the general priesthood of believers I would like to point out:

» First, a functioning priesthood is *essential* and *basic* to the people of God.

» Secondly, any church traditions and practices, which in their practical outworking squelch the functioning of believers as priests must be rejected.

» Thirdly, we must realize that *people*, not buildings, consti- tute the "house of God" (1 Cor. 3:9). For example, well- meaning parents say to their children, "be quiet and still, for we are in the house of God." However, "God's house" must not be identified with any building, for this clouds the fact that Christ's people are a "spiritual house." The old covenant emphasis on *places* has passed away because the fulfillment of these types has come in a spiritual *people*, (*cf.* John 4:20-24).

» Fourthly, in light of our priesthood, we cannot give cre- dence to the historical "clergy/laity" distinction. Howard Snyder points this out by saying:

The New Testament simply does not speak in terms of two classes of Christians—"minister" and "laymen"— as we do today. According to the Bible, the people ("laity" from the Greek: *laos*) of God comprise all Christians, and all Christians through the exercise of spiritual gifts have some "work of ministry." So if we wish to be biblical, we will have to say that all Christians are laymen (God's people) and all are ministers. The "clergy/laity" dichotomy is unbiblical and therefore invalid. It grew up as an accident of church history and actually marked a drift away from biblical faithfulness.... It is one of the principal obstacles to the Church effectively being God's agent of the Kingdom today because it creates the false idea that only "holy men," namely, ordained ministers, are really qualified and responsible for leadership and significant ministry (*The Community of the King* [IVP, 1977], pp. 94-95).

The NT indeed, distinguishes between elders and people (Phil. 1:1). But this distinction *assumes* the priesthood of believers, and does not swallow it up as the "clergy/laity" practice has in the past.

Ephesians 5:18-21

In v. 18, Paul issues forth an imperative, "be filled with the Spirit." The fullness of the Spirit, then, comes to expression through the five participles, which follow: "*speaking* to yourselves...*singing*...*making melody*...*giving thanks*...*submitting yourselves* one to another" (vv. 19-21). The "Spirit-filled" life is not some nebulous, ecstatic experience. It comes to visible expression *in relationship with other people*.

Thus, a basic aspect of our priesthood in Christ is to be in a submissive frame of heart with reference to the other saints. That is to say, wrapped up in our priesthood is a spiritual commitment to others. Before Paul moves on to specific forms of submission, (*cf.* Eph. 5:22; 6:1; 6:5), he first sets forth *the absolute necessity of mutual submission to one another in the fear of Christ* (5:21). Our

Christian priesthood, then, means at least two things: (1) that we make a commitment of love to minister to our brother's or sister's spiritual welfare; and (2) that we submit ourselves to the ministry of our fellow believers for our own edification. Biblical submission, in light of our priesthood, is two-way, not one-way.

1 Corinthians 12: 4-26 (*cf.* Rom. 12:3-8)

In this context, Paul gave a proper perspective on gifts of ministry within the body—a perspective, which many Corinthian believers had forgotten. Let us list Paul's basic points:

1. All believers possess the Spirit of Christ (v. 13).

2. This common Spirit works in all believers (vv. 4-7).

3. The goal of spiritual gifts is mutual edification (vv. 7, 11).

4. The church is a body, whose members all have a vital function (vv. 12, 15-18, 21-22).

5. Ministry in the church does not focus in *one* member, but *many* (vv. 14, 19; *cf.* Appendix).

6. The many members, because of their personal union with Christ, have a living relationship with one another (vv. 12, 25-26).

7. The body cannot function without its parts, and the functioning—priesthood—of the parts is necessary for the unity of the body (vv. 17, 25, 27).

The body brought into existence by Christ's work does absolute justice to both the worth of each individual part, and to the corporate body as a whole. That is to say, the individual is not swallowed up in the body, and the body is not sacrificed for the sake of the individual parts. Just as in a human body, it functions *as a unified whole*, but is *dependent* upon the proper functioning of all the parts. All of this takes on special meaning when the general priesthood of believers is supposed. The body is not meant to depend upon the function of *one* member (vv. 14, 19), while the other members are *passively receptive*. On that basis the body will be crippled, and perhaps die.

It is not going too far, then, to say that the "body" nature of Christ's people is most basic in the NT as Erroll Hulse observes, "the main New Testament analogies describe the Church as a body made up of living members. The analogy of the human body predominates" (*Local Church Practice*, p. 56). Howard Snyder comments that "the Church is no mere collection of isolated individuals, but...it has a corporate or communal nature, which is absolutely essential to it[s] true being" (*The Community of the King*, p. 58).

Ephesians 4:11-16

In this passage the exalted Christ, leading captivity captive, gave gifts to his people (v. 8). Here, we are primarily concerned with the "pastor-teacher" gift of v. 11. In the Puritan tradition, verses 11-12 have been taken to mean that Christ has given pastors and teachers ("doctors"):

> (1) for perfecting the saints; (2) for the work of the ministry; and (3) for the building up of the body of Christ ("A True Description...of the Visible Church," [1589], *The Reformation of the Church*, Iain Murray, ed., p. 200; Owen, *True Nature*, pp. 46-47; "The Form of Presbyterial Church Government," [1645], *The Reformation of the Church*, p. 209). With this interpretation, the entire edification process fell upon the shoulders of "the officers" (*cf.* Thomas Goodwin, *Works*, Vol. 11, p. 310).

However, this interpretation does not appear to be accurate. The King James translation has in v. 12, "for...for...for." But there is in the Greek a change in prepositions not reflected in this rendering. The Greek original has *pros...eis...eis* ["for... unto...unto"]. Thus, this verse can be rendered, "He gave...pastors-teachers *for* equipping the saints *unto* the work of ministry, *unto* the up-building of the body of Christ." In other words, the function of the pastors-teachers is to equip the saints so that *they can minister*.

This construction is further borne out in the context. Verse 16 reveals Christ as joining the whole body together. The emphasis here, as in 1 Corinthians 12, falls on the *total body ministry*, not on the *exclusive ministry of pastors*. The elders' function is a part of the edification process. But the broader body ministry for edification is specifically mentioned two times in v. 16: (1) "every joint supplies"; (2) "in the measure of every part." Thus, edification is not conceived of as being achieved by the ministry of *one part* (the "pastor"), but by the mutual ministry of *every part*.

In summing up this general NT perspective, we can say that:

> All believers are 'ministers' (believer-priests) who have been gifted by God so that they may lovingly build up their spiritual brothers and sisters....each Christian has received a spiritual gift...A gift is a special ability given graciously by God to each person in Christ's Body to help others toward spiritual maturity (*Sixteen Tests of An Authentic New Testament Church*, Fellowship Bible Church [1980], p. 25).

In light of this, the service of elders and deacons must be viewed against the backdrop of the general priesthood of believers. They serve a role in the edification of the body; but they do not constitute the only sources of edification in the body. More will be said on this in the historical section.

The Specific Perspective: "Build Up One Another, Even As You Are Doing" (1 Thess. 5:11)

1 Corinthians 14—"Each of you." Some have shied away from this passage because it includes elements—like "tongues"—which they feel have ceased. Whatever the case may be, however, it seems to me that there are some principles revealed here that confirm the lines of thought we have seen in 1

Corinthians 12, Romans 12, and Ephesians 4:16 (*cf.* Owen, *Works*, Vol. 13, p. 35).

Several things are evident in this chapter. First, Paul is dealing with the entire church *as gathered*: "the whole church come together in one place" (v. 23: *cf.* 1 Cor. 11:18). Secondly, there is *nothing* said about the ministry of *one* person. Thirdly, there is *much* stated about the ministry of many: "that you all may prophesy" (v. 1); "when you come together, every one of you has a psalm, has a teaching, has a revelation, has an interpretation" (v. 26); "you all may prophesy one by one, that all may learn, and all may be comforted" (v. 31).

The Greek word for "each one" is *hekastos*. It is used in the NT to show the *individuality* of judgment: "everyone shall give account of himself to God" (*cf.* Rom. 14:12; *cf.* Matt. 16:27; 25:15; Rom. 2:6). In Acts 2:3, the Holy Spirit "sat upon *each of them*," indicating that this happened to each of the 120 men and women. Does it not appear, then, that the edification of the body involves a *hekastatic* principle? That is, the "ministry" is not given to one person, but to "each of you." This does not mean, of course, that at every gathering each person must participate verbally. But it does at least mean that the time together at some point was open to those who had something from the Lord to contribute (*cf.* Appendix with Barclay's Comments).

We must keep in mind that this "each one" principle was taking place *in the assembling together of the church*: "when you come together [as a church, v. 23], every one of you..." (v. 26). It is, therefore, of note that in the Reformed tradition the minister and his sermon became the focus of attention, and the saints speaking to one another was to take place *in homes apart from the gathering of the church together* (*cf.* Owen, *Works*, Vol. 13, p. 46; Colin Richards, "Fellowship in the Local Church," *Local Church Practice*, pp. 97-98). On what NT basis may we remove the "each of you" practice from the stated "whole church" gatherings? In the Reformed tradition, "the acts of worship were grouped around the pulpit as the most important centre of the church" (J. L. Ainslie, *The Doctrines of Ministerial Order in the*

Reformed Churches of the 16th and 17th Centuries [Edinburgh, 1940], p. 51). Where in 1 Corinthians 14 can we find a pulpit centrality that focuses on one person?

I am not suggesting in all of this that elders never teach in the church gatherings, or, conversely, that *all* must speak. But it is clear that speaking words of edification in the local church is not *limited* to one "minister." Where is *any* opportunity given to others to speak unto edification in our services? What grounds are there in the NT to limit public speaking to the elders, especially the "pastor"? 1 Corinthians 14 teaches the *exact opposite* of such an idea. Are the basic perspectives of this passage now obsolete because the canon of Scripture is closed?

Some may feel that the *hekastatic* practice opens the door for confusion and chaos. But the Corinthian church was *practicing* an "each of you" ministry, and Paul does not censure them for *that*. For Paul, there was no tension between peace and "all prophesy one by one, that all may learn, and all may be comforted" (vv. 31, 33). Thus, to draw back from this principle by erecting a straw man such as, "imagine the confusion if every individual believer claimed his own vision or his own direct leading!" is to evade the teaching of 1 Corinthians 14 (Erroll Hulse, *Local Church Practice*, p. 36). This question must be faced: given the "each of you" principle in 1 Corinthians 14—on what basis can we suggest that edification "is conveyed primarily through [Jesus'] work as a prophet as He instructs the churches through the messengers [the pastors]," (*Ibid.*, p. 36)?

To summarize 1 Corinthians 11-14, we can note:

> The essential activities of the church when gathered are (1) teaching, (2) edification through mutual ministries and (3) worship through the Lord's Supper, singing and prayer.... The meetings of the church should be characterized by the participation of many who are being prompted by the Holy Spirit (*Sixteen Tests*, pp. 13, 27).

Romans 15:14—Nouthetic Interaction

Here Paul gives a commendation to the church at Rome. They were "able also to admonish one another." The word "admonish" (Greek: *noutheteo*) usually means to lovingly confront a sinful act or attitude with truth. The duty of admonishing extends to all the priests. These brothers and sisters were "able" to admonish one another. This implies that this is a skill, which is *learned*. Relating this back to Ephesians 4:11-12, we can see a specific instance here of how the elders are to "equip" the saints: they are to help train the general priesthood in the ability of "admonishing." Could Paul come among our churches today and see visible evidence that the brethren at large were "able" to help one another in this way? If admonishing is left to the elders, then it is no wonder that the saints are ill prepared for this important task. It is in such a realm as this that pastors and teachers are to equip the saints for the work of ministry. I do not see how such training can materialize if edification is conceived of as emanating from only one person's ministry.

1 Thessalonians 4:18; 5:11-14 —Constant Interaction

Paul here focuses on the *mutual ministry* of Christians to one another. The hope all Christians possess is a solid basis upon which to "comfort one another" (4:18). In 5:11, Paul mentions that they *practice*, as an on-going ministry, the building up of one another: "even as you are doing." Again, we are forced to ask, can we meaningfully relate this vital practice to what transpires in churches today? If the brethren rarely see each other during the week, and if the structure of the services focuses on the "pastor," how can we expect this mutual ministry to come to concrete expression?

I suggest here, and will expand on it later, that the reason "one another" ministries are so stifled is precisely because our practice flows out of the conviction that edification comes about through pastoral ministry: "on this office [the "pastor"] and the discharge of it He hath laid the whole weight *of the order, rule, and edification of His church*" (Owen, *True Nature*,

p. 55). The "pastor" becomes the sole source of edification. Thus, according to Goodwin, even when "ordinary" saints converse with one another, the focal point was to be "what it was in a sermon that God blessed to them" (*Works*, Vol. 11, p. 357). But in the NT there is just as much emphasis, if not more, on the profitability of mutual ministry among the general priesthood. Yet this is left untouched and undeveloped in such treatises.

Historically, the duty of mutual edification has been relegated to something that is "occasional," while for Paul "one another" ministry was the basic fabric of body life. Further, this mutual ministry was apparently expressed in the church gatherings ("each of you"), but the Reformed tradition has pushed it outside of such meetings.

In vv. 12-13, Paul makes a clear distinction between the saints and their leaders. Those who have been recognized by the people of God as "elders" are to be "known" and "highly esteemed." While this distinction is clear enough, it does not seem to me that our conception of it is very clear. This distinction has been taken to mean that the elders *do everything*—admonishing, teaching, etc. But we have already seen in Romans 15:14, and can see here in 1 Thessalonians 5:11,14 that there is a general mutual ministry that saints are to perform among themselves.

After giving the general responsibility of edifying one another in verse 11, Paul tells the saints in verse 14 that there are specific needs in the body to which they must minister. Again, Paul does not relegate this "warning/comforting/supporting" ministry to the leaders, but makes it incumbent upon the body to have the same care for one another (*cf.* 1 Cor. 12:25).

Perhaps some would try to find in verse 20, "despise not prophesying," a reference to the centrality of one person's preaching. However, it must be remembered that in 1 Corinthians 14:31 Paul stated: "you may all prophesy one by one, that all may learn, and all may be comforted."

Hebrews 10:24-25

In Hebrew 3:6-14 and 10:24-29 we are faced with the sober reality that there is no place in the Christian profession for slothfulness. In both contexts apostasy is set forth as the alternative for those who neglect the gospel. But, also, in both places the *same mutual duty* is given as the God-ordained means of *restraining* apostasy and *maintaining* perseverance: "*exhort one another* daily...lest any of you be hardened through the deceitfulness of sin (3:13)....not forsaking the assembling [as a church; Greek: *episunagogen*]...but *exhorting* [one another] (10:25)." In the process of the saints' perseverance, then, *a mutual responsibility* stands as the primary revealed method of abiding in Christ and His house.

I dare say that there are too many professing Christians who have never considered the importance of the ministry of other believers in their lives. We live in a society where it is "every person for himself," and the whole idea of mutual dependence is foreign to our thinking. In light of the Hebrews 3:13 and 10:25 perspective, can we not see why it is important to *practice* the "one another"/"each of you" ministry *in our gatherings as a church?*

Hebrew 10:25, of course, is cited as a basis for people to "come to church." It is probably the strongest passage on such a responsibility in the NT But what, according to Hebrews 10:24-25, is to occur in our assembling? Where in 10:25 can you find the idea that we are to come to hear the ministry of *the pastor?* We probably assemble together, but do our services allow for the *exhorting of one another?* If we are going to employ Hebrews 10:25 to press the duty of assembling together, must we not also use it as a guide for what transpires in our gatherings? In light of our way of getting together, it appears that we use about half of the verse rightly—to "assemble," but bury the other half—to "exhort" one another.

For example, Puritan Thomas Goodwin, in discussing the "communion of saints, which the members of a church ought to have with one another," states that, indeed, mutual care "is a constant duty, and that we ought to seek all occasions of act-ing it" (*Works*, Vol. 11, p. 355). However, conceiving of the church gatherings as focusing on the minister and the sermon, and believing that "in private occasional converse, one member may not have opportunity to discourse with another once in seven years," Goodwin suggested that a separate "fixed meet-ing" was necessary, where the brethren could "know one anoth-er's cases and experiences" (*Works*, Vol. 11, p. 353). "The duty enjoined" in Hebrews 10:24, he says, "is a duty distinct from assembling together, which follows in the next verse [10:25]" (*Works*, Vol. 11, p. 354). Thus, while the NT *connects* mutual ministry and our gatherings *as ekklesia*, we have in our practice *separated* them without exegetical basis. Why? Because we have structured our "corporate public worship" around the "pastor," and thereby relegated any mutual ministry to occasional meet-ings, perhaps "once a month" (Colin Richards, "Fellowship," pp. 91, 96, 97).

In light of 1 Corinthians 12:23, 26, 31 and Hebrews 10:24-25, is it not time that we either acknowledge the discrepancy or justify our practice? The traditional "order of service" appears to be at odds with the "each of you" perspective of the NT. Unfortunately it ends up focusing on one ministry, and not on the body. To graphically illustrate this, observe the elements in public worship as articulated by the Westminster Divines in 1645:

> The ordinances in a single congregation are, prayer, thanksgiving, and singing of psalms, the word read, (al-though there follow no immediate explication of what is read) the word expounded and applied, catechizing, the sacraments administered, collection made for the poor, dismissing the people with a blessing ("The Form of Presbyterial Church Gov't.," p. 216).

Everything in this order is done by the "pastor" and other officers, except the "singing of psalms." This is essentially what we still practice today. Does this practice reflect a sensitivity to the glimpses of church gatherings we see in the NT or is it at odds with them? It seems to me that we have made *normative* that for which there is no Scriptural warrant (emphasis on pulpit ministry), and we have *omitted* that for which there is ample Scriptural support (emphasis on one another).

Let us now come to some historical considerations that will help explain why we have come to such questionable practices.

THE HISTORICAL PERSPECTIVE: PRIORITY OF THE "PASTOR"

In this section I wish briefly to trace the historical development of church government, which came to center in the "pastor" as the primary source of edification in the local church.

The Early Period—"The ministry in the Christian Church at the beginning was humble in outward condition and of the simplest in official character. In the course of the centuries it changed greatly" (Ainslie, p. 1).

The Medieval Period—"We see that a great and imposing ecclesiastical organization has come into being. The officials of the Church, the clergy as they have come to be called, form a distinct class, separated from the ordinary people or laity" (Ainslie, p. 1).

The Reformation Period—"In the midst of, and facing, such ecclesiastical conditions, with the ministry of the Church become such as we have seen it, the Reformation Movement of the sixteenth century arose....There is one noteworthy fact at once to be noticed. The Reformers...when renouncing, and opposing themselves to, the Pope and his hierarchy, and setting aside the Medieval Church Orders, did not in the least reject a ministerial order and seek to abolish the Ministry as an institution in the Christian Church....they believed in its immense importance and divine sanction" (Ainslie, pp. 2,5).

I am going to suggest that the evidence from history reveals the swallowing up of a functioning priesthood of believers by the exaltation of this "ministerial order" in the Reformed tradition. It was among the Anabaptists that a more Biblical emphasis on mutual ministry surfaced" (Snyder, *The Community of the King*. pp. 35-36).

First of all, we must understand that territorial and political considerations were wrapped up in the institution of the Reformed ministerial order (Ainslie, pp. 16,60). Just as the Protestants ended up instituting their national churches in competition with the established Romish churches, so the Reformed ministerial order was specifically implemented to take the place of the Papal church order (*cf.* Ainslie, pp. 11, 41, 56). I believe that reckoning with this point helps us to see that, once the Papal order was rejected, a potential vacuum was left. The Protestant "ministerial order" filled this vacuum. Whether or not this order was the right answer is for us to determine in the light of Scripture.

Next, we must see that in the 17th century treatises on church life, two clear trends emerge. These trends are seen in two of the major works on church government by John Owen and Thomas Goodwin. The first trend was an exaltation of "officers." Owen saw "the due performance of the duties" Christ required "brought into this estate by the setting, fixing, or placing *officers* in it" (*True Nature*, p. 41; *cf.* p. 99 where a thriving church life is connected to "a multiplication of elders"). Thomas Goodwin identifies officers as the "furniture" of a house, and thus "when you have officers and ordinances dispensed *by them*, then you have a further presence, He will come down oftener amongst you. The more of ordinances, the more of Christ, the more officers, the more of ordinances" (*Works*, Vol. 11, p. 311, emphasis mine). This emphasis on officers, as Ainslie observed, has "largely persisted to the present day" (p. 15; *cf.* p. 34).

In light of all the emphasis we have seen on *mutual* ministry in the Epistles, the space given to "officers" in Reformed treatises must be designated as inordinate.

This brings us to the second discernable trend. With all the emphasis on "officers," the 17th century treatises on the church have virtually nothing on the "each of you"/"one another" ministries in the local church. Out of 546 pages on church order,

Goodwin has six pages on "communion of saints." In John Owen's *True Nature of A Gospel Church*, he alludes to mutual ministry just a few times (*cf.* pp. 45,93; a four-page sermon on "The Mutual Care of Believers Over One Another" appears in his *Works*, Vol. 16, pp. 477-480, where he begins by seeing the church as "compacted together by officers and ordinances"; and in Vol. 13, pp. 19-49, he carefully delimits what "ordinary," "uncalled" [to the "ministry"] believers may do as ''priests'').

I think it is proper to make the general observation that the post-Reformation tradition, with its almost exclusive emphasis on "officers," had the practical effect of stifling a functioning priesthood of believers. It is important for us to realize, therefore, that we have been heavily influenced by this "officer" oriented tradition, and that the NT data calls for a close scrutiny of that tradition. Just how this tradition has ill-affected us I hope will become more evident as we proceed.

Four Office View

Arising out of this "officer" orientation came a more specific focus on the one person called the "pastor." There emerged in the Reformed tradition a *four*-office view. The "pastor," the "doctor," the "ruling elders," and the "deacons" were conceived of as the expression of church order (*cf.* "A True Description...," pp. 198-199; "The Form of Presbyterial Church Government," pp. 209-214). Let us briefly consider each one, and then come back to expand on the office of "pastor."

The "Doctor"

The "doctor" was made equivalent to the "teacher" mentioned in Ephesians 4:11 and 1 Corinthians 12:28. The "doctor" was distinguished from the "pastor" in that the former was more facile in doctrinal matters, while the latter was more apt in practical matters (Presbyterial Church Gov't., p. 213). Here, we have the basic rationale for seminary professors, as the Westminster

Divines stated that this "doctor is of most excellent use
in schools and universities" (*Ibid.*, p. 213).

The "Ruling Elders"

These are men who "join with the minister [pastor] in
the government of the church" (*Ibid.*, p. 214). Thus,
the office of elder was divided up, based mainly on an
arbitrary interpretation of I Timothy 5:17, into the
"teaching/ruling" elder (the "pastor" who labors in the
Word), and "ruling elders." I say this use of I Timothy
5:17 is arbitrary because it introduces an artificial distinction among elders. *All elders* must be "apt to teach,"
and all elders are to "rule." To be sure, there is in I
Timothy 5:17 a distinction among the elders. But it is a
distinction of *comparative time given*, not a distinction
of *office*. The ones who labor in the Word are part of a
broader body of elders, *all* of whom are potentially worthy of financial support. There is in the text no warrant
to elevate one man as the "pastor"—who is supported
financially—and *separate* him from the other "elders."
E.W. Johnson sums up the matter this way: "A church
cannot be taught except it be ruled, and a church cannot be ruled except it be taught.... I do not believe in
a distinction between ruling elders and teaching elders"
(*Sovereign Grace Message*, July, 1977, p. 4; *cf. BRR*, 7:2,
p. 30). Our *practice* would translate I Timothy 5:17,
"Let the elders who rule assist the fully-supported pastor who teaches *and* rules." Here again, we can see how
the elevation of the "pastor" not only stifles the general
priesthood, it also stifles the proper functioning of the
eldership. The "ruling elders" become simply the "long
arms" of the "pastor" (Ainslie, pp. 63-64).

The "Deacons"

The deacons are to care for the material aspects of church
life. But the Westminster Divines made it clear that the
deacons were "not to preach the word, or administer the

sacraments" ("Form," p. 214). Such dogmatism is in contradiction with the ministry of "deacon" Philip (Acts 6:2-5), who both preached publicly and baptized many people (Acts 8:5,12).

The "Pastor"

In contrast to the NT focus on mutual ministry, the Puritans focused on the "pastor." Owen confidently asserted, "on this office [pastor] and the discharge of it He hath laid the whole weight of the *order, rule, and edification of His church*" (*True Nature*, p. 55). Remember, he is not saying on the *plurality of eldership* rests the rule of the church. It is upon the *one person* who occupies the separate office of "pastor." Since our practice generally corresponds with this notion, we must reflect upon this question: *where in the NT can we demonstrate that the edification of the church has been committed to the ministry of one part of the body, especially in light of 1 Corinthians 12:14,19,31, and Hebrews 10:24-25?*

What authority, privileges and duties were attached to the office of "pastor"? Much detail will be given here in order to show that this one-man centrality effectively squelched the priesthood of believers. If all edification is attributed to one source, then the many members, practically speaking, have no function. They become passive recipients, not active priests.

"The Power of the Keys"

First, to the "pastor" alone was given "the power of the keys" (*cf.* Ainslie, pp. 61, 66). These "keys" were exercised "by preaching and carrying out Church Discipline" (*cf.* Ainslie, p.67). Thus, "only ministers...were to preach publicly" (*cf.* Ainslie, p. 69). When preaching, they usually wore a black gown (*Ibid.*, p. 37). The act of one man preaching the Word became the focal point of the church gatherings (*Ibid.*, pp. 49,59). It is no wonder, then, that "in the interior of a Protestant Church, the pulpit has always been the principal piece of furniture" (*Ibid.*, quoting Dr.

Pannier, p. 50). But we must ask: in 1 Corinthians 14 is a *singular* or *multiple* ministry emphasized? Where in the NT can we observe "that the acts of worship were grouped around the pulpit as the most important centre of the church" (*Ibid.*, p. 51)? Preaching in the Reformed tradition, notes Ainslie, "became something of a sacramental act and greater than the sacramental symbols of the Communion" (p. 52).

Discipline came to be non-centralized in the hands of the "pastor," for obvious reasons (*Ibid.*, pp. 73-74). Nevertheless, in practice the "pastor" came to dominate in the disciplinary procedure (*Ibid.*, pp. 76-77,85,87-88). The reason the "pastor" was so dominant in the worship service was because they believed he had a special "ministry unto edification" (*cf.* Owen, *True Nature*, pp. 42,55), which was given to no one else. For example, Goodwin observed that the edification of the church was extremely important, "for there is a fullness of stature appointed, and every member must grow up unto it before they go to heaven" (*Works*, Vol. 11, p. 300). But he viewed this edification process as coming through "officers," not through "one another" (*Ibid.*, pp. 311-312). Interestingly, and perhaps expectedly, Goodwin must, in pressing home the *need* for the "pastor," deny the sufficiency of the Spirit-anointing each believer possesses (*cf.* 1 John 2:20, 27).

> By these officers he buildeth the house more and more.... The more ordinances, the more of Christ; the more of officers, the more of ordinances....Because the church is under age [Eph. 4:13] therefore she is to have these officers over her until she comes to a perfect man, and to the full stature. And children under age, now as well as then, are to be under tutors and governors, Galatians 4:2...he contented not himself to have them enjoy such occasional means as the brethren in communion were able to afford each other... but he would farther have men of the best and eminentest gifts set apart usually unto it.... Yea, further, the apostle otherwise intimates that without men being set apart unto it there would

be no preserving of knowledge, but the ordinary sort
of believers would have been exposed to the danger of
being carried away by seducers...for ordinary sort of believers, being children not fully grown up, would easily
have been seduced, if they had not had guides...if this
business had been in common left to the common care
of every member watching over each other, there would
have been a defect (*Works*, Vol. 11, pp. 310-314).

You can see how there is here a functional disdain for the
mutual ministries, but an all-sufficiency attributed to one person's ministry.

"Administer the Sacraments"

Not only was the "pastor" the only one who could preach publicly,
but this person was also the only one who could "administer the
sacraments" (Owen, *True Nature*, p. 68; Ainslie, pp. 56,63,65;
Owen, *Works*, Vol. 13, p. 43; Goodwin, *Works*, Vol. 11, p. 309). I
have a real problem with this idea that "pastors" are the exclusive
"dispensers of the sacraments." The background of this idea that
only certain men are qualified to administer the ordinances of the
church is very suspect, and reeks of magical notions about the
elements (*cf.* Leonard Verduin, *The Reformers and Their Stepchildren*, pp. 154-158). From reading the NT, you would get the
impression that the Lord's Supper was a *meal* shared among the
saints, not something to be formally "administered."

"Read the Scriptures Publicly"

The Westminster Divines taught that only the "pastor" could
read the Scriptures publicly (*cf.* Form, p. 210). Three Old Testament contexts are cited as proof "that the public reading of the
Scriptures belongeth to the pastor's office."

"Rules for Examination."

Obviously, the man to occupy this exalted office of "pastor"
must have distinctive qualifications. After Owen outlined the
duties of the "pastor," it is not surprising that he exclaims, "what

learning, labour, study, pains, ability and exercise of the ratio-
nal faculties, are ordinarily required unto the right discharge of
these duties" (*True Nature*, p. 70). More to the point are the
"rules for examination" of potential ministers drawn up by the
Westminster Divines:

> He shall be examined touching his skill in the origi-
> nal tongues, and his trial to be made by reading the
> Hebrew and Greek Testaments, and rendering some
> portion of some into Latin; and if he be defective in
> them, enquiry shall be made more strictly after his other
> learning, and whether he hath skill in logic and phi-
> losophy...What authors in divinity he hath read, and
> is best acquainted...He shall also, within a competent
> time, frame a discourse in Latin upon such a common-
> place or controversy in divinity as shall be assigned to
> him (Form, pp. 226-227)

If these "rules" were translated into first century terminol-
ogy, there would never have been any elders recognized in the
churches, (*cf.* Acts 14:23 and Titus 1:5)! Do we really believe
that such standards were applied to men in the early church? Is it
not safe to believe that many elders in the early days were common folks, mature in the faith, able to meet the inspired standards of 1 Timothy 3:1-7 and Titus 1:6-8, (*cf.* 1 Cor. 1:26-28)?
Must "ordinary pastors and teachers...be more than ordinarily
skilled in their writing" (Goodwin, *Works*. Vol. 11, p. 314)? Why
are such high standards applied to the "teaching/ruling" elders,
but not to the "ruling" elders?

All of this, I believe, has created an artificial standard of
intellectual attainment for "ministers." It explains why there
is emphasis on academics in seminaries. It explains why much
teaching is so involved and intricate that it goes over the head
of the average believer. It explains why believer-priests are afraid
to express their opinions. One brother wrote me recently and,
before setting forth his ideas, apologized with these words: "I
have had no seminary education, and I do not know Greek,

and that causes me to feel a little intimidated." If a man has an anointing of the Spirit, he is spiritually equipped to "test the spirits" and to discern spiritual things (*cf.* 1 Cor. 2:15). All of this accounts for why "ministers" are treated as an elite class, to whom "reverential estimation" is due (Owen, *Works.* Vol. 13, p. 58).

With this emphasis on the "learning" of the "pastor," another unfortunate thing occurred. The "pastor," being "above" the common people, became isolated from any ministry of the people to him. Thus, exhortation and encouragement could come only from other ministers. "Let this whole treatise of discipline be read in the consistory, and let the ministers, elders, and deacons be censured one after another: yet so that the minister concerning doctrine be censured of ministers only" (The Book Of Discipline, [1587] *The Reformation of the Church*, p. 184).

With the "pastor" conceived of as "the eyes of the church," (*True Nature*, p. 59), how did the Puritans deal with mutual ministry? Obviously, they confessed the "priesthood of all believers," and believed that believers had mutual responsibilities. However, it is clear that the pervasive centrality of the "pastor" thwarted any meaningful expression of mutual ministry in the church. When Owen and Goodwin deal with this subject, you get the feeling that the "common" brethren would have a cloud hanging over their heads for fear of "intruding into the pastor's office" (*A True Description*, p. 200). Owen sets out "to show...what remaineth for the rest of God's people to do, for their own and others' edification" (*Works*, Vol. 13, pp. 19-20). Of course, he rules out mutual ministry occurring during the meetings of the church (*cf.* vol. 13, p. 43). He allows for "cases extraordinary" where an "uncalled" Christian may "teach and declare the faith to others." But "for such an undertaking [he] must have a warrant by an immediate call from God," and Owen goes on to elaborate three ways in which such a call may be discerned (*cf.* vol. 13, pp. 28-29). Further, "uncalled Christians" may search the Scriptures diligently (*cf.* vol. 13, p. 39). They may also judge by the Scriptures the doctrine they hear publicly (*cf.* vol. 13, p. 40). Here we must wonder how most "uncalled" Christians would feel about questioning the learned "ministers," especially since they were taught that such men "were to be heard as if it were God Himself speaking" (Ainslie, p. 48). There would surely be a marked hesitancy to raise questions about what they heard publicly from the Puritan giants.

Next, the "uncalled Christian," Owen said, has "one another" duties. He gives several qualifications as to when and how such duties are to be performed, (*cf.* vol. 13. pp. 43-45). Common believers must be careful, for example, about "opening" Scripture, for "there is much difference between opening or interpreting the word, and *applying* the word upon the advantage of such an approved interpretation" (vol. 13, p. 44). The *approved interpretation* must mean that which has come from the "pastor." Nothing could be more detrimental to the priesthood of all believers than to suggest that one person gives out "approved interpretations" of Scripture, which "uncalled" brethren *cannot produce*. Thus, he suggests that in order for mutual ministry to be "for the better, and not for the worse, observe these things":

1. Have two or three families meet in a home (*cf.* vol. 13, p. 46), where they may:

2. Pray together, (*cf.* vol. 13, p. 46);

3. Comfort and strengthen one another "with the same consolations and promises, which, by *the benefit of the public ministry*, they have received from the word" (vol. 13, p. 46: emphasis mine);

4. "Apply unto and instruct one another in the word of God, doing it as a charitable duty, and not out of necessary function" (Vol. 13, p. 46);

5. "The people of God are allowed all quiet and peaceable means, whereby they may help one another forward in the knowledge of godliness" (Vol. 13, p. 47).

He closes by making it clear that "interpreting the word" belongs only to the "ministers," while "applying" the word belongs to the common believer (Vol. 13, p. 49). Owen cites with approval Rutherford's words of 1641: "Our assembly also, commandeth godly conference at all occasional meetings, or as God's providence shall dispose, as the word commandeth, providing none invade the pastor's office, to preach the word, who are not called thereunto by God and His church" (Vol. 13, p. 49).

Goodwin basically follows this same pattern, and emphasized that mutual care "does not properly consist in the communications of such gifts, whereby the church is edified in the public worship of God" (Vol. 11, p. 357).

One can easily see in all this that the "pastor's" ministry dominates the public gatherings, and even spills over into the private meetings where his sermons comprise the basic subject matter. Also, it can be noted that in Owen's point four above, he does not view mutual teaching as a *necessary function*. However, we have seen from the NT that it is to be the most basic function of the priests in the New Covenant, and that it occurred in the gathered meetings of the church that took place in homes.

DISCUSSION OF ISSUES: THE NEED - A RETURN TO BODY PRIORITY

1. *Do elders constitute Christ's authority in the church?* The Reformed tradition tends to view elders as necessary in order for Christ's authority to be present. David Fountain, for example, says: "The local assemblies were not complete, and needed Christ's authority in their midst by means of Elders...There is no authority in the church properly so-called but rests in the offices of it" ("Authority and Elders," *The Ideal Church*, p. 14). Colin Richards says:

A fellowship of Christians without God appointed officers can hardly be regarded as ideal or complete—and
some would say, and I think with some justification,
that such a fellowship could hardly be considered a
church ("Fellowship" p. 101).

But is this correct? In Acts, elders were ordained in every
"*ekklesia*" (Acts 14:23). The *ekklesia* existed and functioned for a
considerable period before the *elders* were set apart.

The *local church* possesses authority from Christ to rec-
ognize ministries in her midst, and confront sin in her midst
(Matt. 18:17). Paul confronted the Corinthian church as a
whole, not the elders, for their failure to purge out the leaven.
The action to deal with this matter occurred when the church
was "gathered together" (1 Cor. 5:4). In Revelation 2 & 3
Christ deals directly with each church (*cf.* Rev. 22:16). In
Matthew 18:17, matters of discipline are taken "to the church."
The person of Christ is manifested in the assembly, and it is his
will that guides the congregation (*cf.* Matt. 18:20; Eph. 5:24).
And certainly, the church does not turn over its authority to
the officers when they are elected, as Owen suggested (*True
Nature*, pp. 46, 49).

2. *Is there any Scriptural warrant to separate one person as "pastor" in distinction from the other elders?* No. If you have three
elders, you also have three pastors (*cf.* BRR. 7:2, 1978, p. 30).
It is generally admitted that "elder/bishop/pastor" are three
designations of the same function. Tradition has created a separate office of "pastor," set up seminaries to train people for the
"ministry," and presented such persons as the primary source
of edification in the local church. The Scripture views elders as
a *body* (Acts 20:17, 28). The charge to feed the body comes
to *all* elders, not just to those who "labour in the word and
doctrine." In our practice we end up with two kinds of elders,
and one (intellectually higher) set of standards is applied to
one, and another set for the *others*. On what Biblical basis do
we practice this?

3. *Is there any Scriptural warrant for one person's ministry to be the center-point of church gatherings?* No. There is no evidence anywhere in the NT for the centrality of *one member's* ministry (*cf.* 1 Cor. 14:14, 19, 31). Rather, to the contrary, there is abundant evidence in the NT of *multiple participation* in the church gatherings (*cf.* 1 Cor. 14:31). Again, it appears that we have made normative that for which there is no evidence (one person's ministry), and we have abandoned that for which there is *copious* evidence ("each of you," 1 Cor. 14:26).

4. *Does this mean that everyone should speak in the public gatherings?* Over a period of time, *Yes.* We should seek to capture the spirit of the NT and have an open meeting with mutual participation, mutual interaction, and opportunity for questioning of those who may teach the Word. Why? Because the NT emphasizes that our cleaving to, and growth in Christ, is intimately connected to our mutual ministries to one another. Our speaking to one another is for the purpose of edification, which is synonymous with being built up in Christ (*cf.* Rom. 14:19; 1 Cor. 14:3, 12,26b; 1 Thess. 5:11). The NT presents us with a *functioning priesthood* ministering to one another in the church gathering; our practice reveals virtually no opportunity for saints to mutually minister in our time together. I am simply pleading that we turn from our one-person orientation, and practice *one-anothering.*

5. *But how will Christ reign in our gatherings if one person does not do most of the teaching?* We are probably so used to thinking in terms of one saint's ministry that *one-anothering* is new to us. Therefore, we must orient ourselves to the fact that *the centrality of the Lord must not be equated with the speaking of one person.* The NT nowhere makes this equation. Rather, the congregation is to be edified by learning of Christ from all the saints. The Puritans were aware of the priesthood, but unfortunately their conception of the "pastor" served to suppress the actual functioning of the priesthood at large. Edification from the *body*

is hardly necessary if the "whole weight" of edification rests on the "pastor," as Owen suggested. If God has ordained for us to grow in Christ through *many* functioning priests, then the limiting of edification to *one part* has to be significantly damaging (*cf.* Eph. 4:16).

6. *What, then, are the basic functions of the elders?* They are to oversee the priesthood by: (a) equipping the church so that they can fulfill their ministries (*cf.* Eph. 4:12); this is done by teaching and example; (b) teaching and applying God's Word publicly and privately (*cf.* Acts 20:28). The elders are to act *as a body* not as (1) the "pastor" and (2) the "ruling elders," who act as the "long arms" of the "pastor." The people in this body are *equal in function*, but obviously *differ in the expression of their gifts and in the time they may give* to watching over and feeding the flock.

7. *What is to be gained by moving away from edification being centralized in the "pastor?"* If the NT teaches much about mutual ministry, and nothing about one person's ministry, we will find ourselves blessed in implementing Christ's commandments because we love Him (*cf.* John 14:15; 13:17). If our union with Christ is meant to be nourished particularly by mutual ministries, then we will be strengthened by experiencing them. If our gatherings together as a church are to be maximized unto edification, then this will be gained by "exhorting one another, and speaking to one another in psalms, hymns, and spiritual songs."

Obviously, many would claim that they have been edified in a church by the pastor's ministry. But has Christ *revealed* that we are to be edified by *one* gift or by *many*? Is it Scriptural to attribute the "whole weight" of edification to the "pastor," or not? We will grow by ceasing to be passive priests, and becoming active priests offering spiritual sacrifices to Christ. In light of the fact that pastor-centrality historically has put water on the flames of mutual ministry, we will gain much in Christ by returning to that which is revealed in Scripture.

CONCLUDING REMARKS

1. *We must let the light of the Word shine upon our practice.* Alexander Hay observes: "Tertullian found it necessary to say, 'Custom without truth is error grown old.' There is not a little in our modern church order and practice that has no Scriptural warrant. Yet, because it has long been the custom, it is accepted without question as an essential part of the divine order" (*N.T. Order*, p. 285).

Remember, the Reformed tradition has been very dogmatic in asserting that their "ministerial order" possessed "divine sanction" (*cf.* Ainslie, p. 5). "From the NT and the Scriptures as a whole came the chief formative guidance in the work of instituting the Reformed ministry" (*cf.* Ainslie, p. 13). But just where in the NT is the exegetical warrant for the "pastor-doctor-elders-deacons" view? Where in the NT do we find that Christ has placed the "whole weight" of edification on the ministry of "the pastor"? What are we to do with all the weight of evidence regarding the *mutual ministries?* Must we not see from history a rather clear correlation between the *rise of the "pastor"* and the *demise of one-anothering?* "How does the church actually function compared with what the Word of God says? Is the practical application of Ephesians 4:11 and 1 Corinthians 12:28 even possible in our church given its present structure? If not, what would God have us do?" (Snyder, p. 94).

2. *"We must remember not to be afraid to be adventurous and willing to experiment in church life.* We shall not be reluctant to do this or rash in our actions if we engage in a constant revision of all our activities" (Colin Richards, "Fellowship," p. 99, emphasis mine). Specifically:

> There is the need, too, for audible participation by the congregation. Let the 'Amen' be hearty at the end of the prayers (*cf.* 1 Cor. 14:16). There ought to be opportunities somewhere within the life of the church for prayer and general ministry for all the members of the

local church. Although this is an area that bristles with problems we cannot ignore it or else we are failing to take seriously the words of Paul in 1 Corinthians 14:26 'When ye come together, every one of you has a psalm, has a doctrine, has a tongue, has a revelation, has an interpretation' (Richards, "Fellowship," p. 93).

The people of God must come to the gatherings with *something on their hearts from the Lord* that will edify the others. Our practice has probably trained them to be passive. But the priests must have an opportunity to *function. Provision* must be made for this, which cannot occur if the "pastor" dominates the "order of worship." John McArthur, Jr. makes this astute observation:

> God has given each member certain spiritual gifts for the work of the ministry.... The local church essentially is a training place to equip Christians to carry out their own ministries. Unfortunately, for many Christians the church is a place to go to watch professionals perform and to pay the professionals to carry out the church program. In many quarters Christianity has deteriorated into professional "pulpitism," financed by lay spectators. The church hires a staff of ministers to do all the Christian service. This scheme is not only a violation of God's plan, but an absolute detriment to the growth of the church and the vitality of the members of the body. Every member needs to find a significant place of service. To limit the work of the ministry to a small, select class of full-time clergymen hinders the spiritual growth of God's people, stunts the development of the body, and hinders the evangelistic outreach of the church into the community, (*cf. The Church: The Body of Christ*, pp. 122-123).

3. *We must strive after local churches that visibly minister to one another.* If growth in Christ is the *goal*, then the NT reveals

mutual ministry as a crucial *means* to this end. The goal is for *all the parts* to function (Eph. 4:16). Are our churches marked by the "love" Christ commanded? Jay Adams raises some searching questions for us to consider in this regard:

> The church has virtually lost its image as the loving, forgiving, helping and healing society of people who gather together to "build up one another." There is plenty of talk about the church as the institution in which you can find coldness, and slander, and alienation; but what has happened to her first century image?... Where can you find a church in which the members really "provoke one another to good works"? Where do you find those who are spiritually restoring a brother who is caught in a trespass?... Where in the church do you see the confrontation of brethren who have offended one another taking place (*cf.* Matt. 5:23-24; 18:15-20)?, [*Christ and Your Problems*, pp. 8-9].

Our union with Christ brings us into a *body* (*cf.* 1 Cor. 12:13). Christ saves *individuals,* and then ordains for them to grow in *fellowship with others* (whose gifts and graces they need), not in *isolation.*

We must allow our confidence in Christ to bring with it confidence in our brothers and sisters. Max Weber, in his *The Protestant Ethic and the Spirit of Capitalism* (1905), observes that in Puritanism "the most extreme form of that exclusive trust in God.... comes out for instance in the strikingly frequent repetition, especially in the English Puritan literature, of warnings against any trust in the aid of friendship of men. Even the amiable Baxter exhorts deep distrust of even one's closest friend, and Bailey exhorts to trust no one and to say nothing compromising to anyone. Only God should be your confidant" (p. 106). Contrary to these sentiments, the NT teaches that we are to be open in our relationships with the saints and bear one another's burdens (Gal. 6:2). We should expect the best from the saints, not the *worst* (Philemon 21; 2 Thess. 3:4).

4. *We must realize that functioning more Biblically as a church does not, in and of itself, produce spirituality.* It is the Spirit as the presence of Christ who gives life to the body. Alexander Hay makes this crucial observation:

> The visible forms of the order are without power in themselves; in fact they are such that they cannot stand-alone. It is the presence of Christ in the gathering of the church, the guidance of the Spirit through the prayer of the church, and the gifts of the Spirit manifested through the members of the church, that provide all the wisdom and power and produce all the fruit (*N.T. Order*, p. 297).

5. *We must ask ourselves if our churches are being prepared for future suffering.* Our current "freedoms" with reference to assembling together may be disrupted some day by governmental upheaval. Are the saints being prepared now to care and sacrifice for one another? What if all evangelical pastors were arrested? Would the churches be in a position to continue functioning? The possibility of an underground church in the future—which is a *reality* in many places—should cause us to reflect upon how prepared we are for such a situation. Learning to care for and minister to one another *now* is essential (*cf.* Richard Wurmbrand, *Preparing for the Underground Church*).

6. *We must listen obediently to Christ speaking in Scripture.* It is possible to nullify the Word of God by our traditions. A reluctance to re-examine practices that appear to be contrary to the Word is indication of a party spirit, or a fear of truth. May we with meekness receive the Word and practice it.

Some might feel that churches are not "ready" to practice the *mutuality* that has been discussed in this article. But why should Christ's will be postponed? Were churches "ready" to practice the responsibilities of priesthood a hundred years ago? Fifty? Twenty? If years of tradition are wrong, just when will we be "ready" to edify one another as we should? If something important is missing in our churches, then the time has come for us to implement what Christ has revealed. The implications of a functioning priesthood probably seem "radical" only because we are used to patterns of tradition, which have no foundation in Scripture.

Saints, I have poured out my heart. I ask you now to think about these matters before the Lord and His Word. If you have a word of correction, caution, modification, or encouragement, I want to be receptive to your comments. Remember, my primary concern has been to question the priority of the "pastor" in light of the priority of the *priesthood* in the NT. I believe that the continuance of one-person orientation is the precise area that will hinder us from the one-anothering that is revealed as an essential element of growth in Christ. May the Lord Jesus give us wisdom in these vital areas.

Although there are questionable elements in William Barclay's theology, the following excerpt from *The Letter to the Corinthians* on 1 Corinthians 14 (pp. 149-150) is the best precise summary of the spirit of the NT gatherings that I have ever seen. The sub-headings are not in the original text, and several of my comments will follow the excerpt.

LIBERTY - BUT NOT DISORDER

Paul comes near to the end of this section with some very practical advice. He is determined that anyone who possesses a gift should receive a chance to exercise that gift; but he is equally determined that the services of the Church should not thereby become a kind of competitive disorder. Only two or three are to exercise the gift of tongues, and then only if there is someone there to interpret. All have the gift of forth-telling the truth, but again only two or three are to exercise it; and if someone in the congregation has the conviction that he has received a special message, the man who is speaking must give way to him and give him opportunity to express it. The man who is speaking can perfectly well do so, and need not say that he is carried away by inspiration and cannot stop, because the preacher is able to control his own spirit. There must be liberty but there must be no disorder. The God of peace must be worshipped in peace.

THE CHURCH GATHERED - FREEDOM WITHIN STRUCTURE.

It is true to say that there is no more interesting section in the whole letter than this, for it sheds a flood of light on what a Church service was like in the early Church. There was obviously a freedom and informality about it, which is completely strange to our ideas. From this passage two very great questions emerge.

1. Are pastors the only source of edification?

Clearly the early Church had no professional ministry. True, the apostles stood out with a very special authority; but at this stage the Church had no professional local ministry. It was open to anyone who had a gift to use that gift. Has the Church done rightly or wrongly in instituting a professional ministry? Clearly there is something essential in that, in our busy age when men are so preoccupied with material things, one man should be set apart to live close to God, and to bring his fellow men the truth and the guidance and the comfort, which God gives to him. But on the other hand there is the obvious danger that when a man becomes a professional preacher he is, at least, sometimes, in the position of having to say something when he really has nothing to say. However that may be, it must remain true that if a man has a message to give his fellow men no ecclesiastical rules and regulations should be able to stop him giving it. It is certainly a mistake to think that only the professional ministry can ever bring God's truth to men.

2. Should the priesthood be prepared to function?

There was obviously a flexibility about the order of service in the early Church, which is now totally lacking. There was clearly no settled order at all. Everything was informal enough to allow any man who felt he had a message to give it. It may well be that we have set far too much store on dignity and order nowadays. It may well be that we have become the slaves of orders of service. The really notable thing about an early Church service must have been that almost everyone came feeling that he had both the privilege and the obligation of contributing something to it. A man did not come with the sole intention of being a passive listener. He did not come only to receive, he came also to give. Obviously this had its dangers for it is clear that in Corinth there were those who were too fond of the sound of their own voices; but nonetheless the Church must have been in those days much more the real possession of the ordinary Christian. It may well be that the Church lost something when she delegated so much to the professional ministry, and left so little to the ordinary Church member; and it may well be that the blame lies not with the ministry for annexing those rights, but with the laity for abandoning them. It is all too true that there are many Church members whose attitude is that they think far more of what the Church can do for them than of what they can do for the Church, and who are very ready to criticize what is done, but very unready to take any share in doing the Church's work themselves.

THREE COMMENTS ON BARCLAY'S REMARKS:

1. Barclay's statement that in our "busy age" it is good to have "one man set apart from material things and to live close to God," lacks Scriptural support. Elders are certainly to be supported by the church, but such support is by no means limited to "one man." If possible, the church should financially support as many elders as it can, not because of busy times, but in order to maximize edification in the church (cf. Greg Hufstetler, "The Support of Elders in the NT," *BRR*. 7:2. pp. 46-50). Further, there is no between the description of elders in the NT and the "professional ministry" that has appeared in the history of the church.

2. Some have argued that 1 Corinthians 14 must be "qualified" by later NT revelation. For example, Pastor Al Martin said in this regard that "churches are taking on their more permanent form under the direction of Timothy and Titus... and you see a transition... The directions of Paul with regard to the life of the church at Corinth are materially different from the directions in the Pastoral Epistles" ("Law and Gospel," Delivered in Toronto, Canada, Feb. 11, 1980). Just what is "materially different."? Is 1 Corinthians 14 in some way at variance with 1 and 2 Timothy and Titus? Of course not. Was the Corinthian church functioning without elders when Paul wrote 1 Corinthians 14? We have every reason to believe that they had elders just as did all the other churches.

Thus we can conclude that there is *nothing* incompatible between 1 Corinthians 14 and later NT revelation. The idea that as time elapsed the early church gatherings saw an *increasing* focus on the ministry of elders and a corresponding *decrease* in the ministry of the general priesthood is without Biblical foundation. The *full* ministry of elders is completely compatible with the *full* functioning of the priesthood. But post-apostolic church life quickly moved away from the simplicity of the NT life to a position where the church hierarchy swallowed up the ministry of the spiritual priesthood.

3. As I have studied that matter, it has been of interest to note that commentators generally are agreed on the freedom-within-structure nature of the NT church gatherings. For example, in commenting on James 1:19, "let every one be quick to hear, slow to speak and slow to anger," Curtis Vaughn and Earl Kelly observe:

> There may be an allusion to the free and unstructured worship of early Christian assemblies (*James: A Study Guide*, [Zondervan. 1960] p. 35).

> It is possible that contentious Christian babes were taking advantage of the informal style of worship in the early Christian church to produce wrangling (*James: A Primer for Christian Living*, [Presbyterian & Reformed. 1974] p. 69).

This question must be asked: if it is acknowledged that such structured informality existed in the early church meetings, on what basis do we not practice the basic principles found in 1 Corinthians 14? Why was it *good* for them, but apparently *unworkable* or "dangerous" for us? Does the traditional order of service reflect structured informality, or a closed formality that stifles the priesthood of believers to one another?

— Jon Zens

THE PASTOR

DOES EACH CHURCH NEED "ONE"?

(This article originally was published as an eight-page booklet in 1982)

The following article by Frank Owen appeared in a Kentucky Southern Baptist paper, and no doubt it expresses the thought patterns of many Christians. It accurately summarizes the prevailing ideas about "the pastor":

> *The Old Testament had the prophet and the priest. The priests were generally overseers of the house of worship and administered its ceremonies. The prophets were less formal, free spokesmen—forth-tellers and sometimes foretellers.*
>
> *In Evangelical Christianity the church has merged the two Old Testament figures into one office called "pastor." From the beginning the church was a fellowship of people rather than a "temple." The fellowship was to have a holy place to meet but the church itself, was "Ho Koinonia." This fellowship, like a flock, needed a leader like a shepherd.*
>
> *Israel was a land of flocks and shepherds. From this pastoral setting and the ministry of Jesus, the shepherd and flock relationship became the pattern. That is how we acquired the term "pastor" in relation to the church.*
>
> *Recent history has seen the rapid growth of multiple specialized ministries, especially in larger churches. Assistant pastors, Ministers of Education, Music, Youth etc. Ministers have had to learn to serve together. Lay members have needed to understand the roles of the pastor and the auxiliary ministers.*
>
> *An orderly church needs one overseer, one shepherd, and one pastor. Specialized ministers have their own realms of distinct service but the pastor needs to have general oversight of the education, music, youth, activities and any other ministries in the flock. The church that fails to recog-*

nize and uphold the pastor in this role is apt to lack unity
in its sense of direction, and is risking serious personnel
problems with an unsupervised staff.

I have heard a few argue that each ministry should
be separate, parallel and independent of each other. Al-
low this old veteran to observe that chaos easily develops
where no one is in charge. If the church is to be one flock, it
needs one shepherd. Let him be the first among equals. He
must be wise to magnify his associates and their work – let
them stand tall. He needs to be humble, gentle and loving
with those whom he supervises, but he must not abdicate
his Biblically-based assignment to oversee the church. Wise
church members will encourage this, (Western Recorder,
January 14, 1981; used with permission).

I would like to reflect on this article in the *light of Scripture.*

I believe that the ideas Mr. Owen sets forth are absolutely
indefensible from God's Word. They express very well the *tradi-*
tion of men, but they utterly fail to reflect *NT teaching.*

Please *think* with me as we examine Mr. Owen's reasoning. I
do not challenge these common notions in order to be a "trou-
blemaker." Rather, I believe we are "peacemakers" by pursuing
Biblical perspectives. Therefore I challenge this article because
if this position is wrong, it means that our practice is wrong.
And if our practice is wrong in such a crucial area, then we are
in disobedience to Christ's revealed will. But Christ's sheep are
sensitive to His voice in Scripture (*cf.* John 10:4-5, 27). If our
disobedience is *uncovered* by the light of the Scripture, then we
need to *change.*

If we do not care what Christ says about local church life, or
if we do not want to change when new understanding comes,
there is something seriously wrong with our hearts. Brothers and
sisters, I pray that our consciences will be sensitive to Christ's
precious Word, and that we will find joy in *doing* what our Lord
commands (*cf.* John 14:17; 15:10-11).

Let us examine Mr. Owen's remarks.

1. Mr. Owen asserts that "Evangelical Christianity...has merged the two Old Testament figures [of prophet and priest] into one office called 'pastor.'" On what Scriptural basis has this been done? First of all, *Christ* is the primary reference of the Old Testament figures of prophet, priest, and king. *He* is the prophet Moses spoke of who would be raised up (*cf.* Deut.18:15,18); He is the priest who offered Himself for our sins (*cf.* Heb. 5:5; 7:21,24); He is the king over His people (*cf.* Heb. 7:2; Rev. 17:14).

These Old Testament figures were first of all *types of Christ*. Also, the great leaders, like Moses, Joshua and Elijah, are not types of one-man leadership in the church, but again, they are *types of Christ*.

Further, the "priest" figure in the Old Testament is, in the gospel age, fully realized in the *priesthood of all believers* (*cf.* 1 Peter 2:5, 9), not in "the pastor." Only a few men were priests under the old covenant; now *all* believers—men, women, and children—are priests before God and to one another.

Indeed, elders can be viewed as *under*shepherds (*cf.* 1 Peter 5:4). However, Mr. Owen's point is that there is to be only *one shepherd*—i.e., "the pastor." But the NT always views these undershepherds in the local church as plural "pastors," never as singular "pastor" (*cf.* Acts 20:17; James 5:14). *Not one example can be shown from the NT where a church had "one" pastor.* On what Biblical basis, therefore, have we created the office of *one* pastor?

2. Mr. Owen avers that each local church "like a flock, needed a leader like a shepherd." However, the NT teaches that the only (*singular*) Shepherd we have is *Christ* (*cf.* John 10:11-14; 1 Peter 5:4). Christ is the Head of the church, and He gives a plurality of pastors to share in the oversight of each local church. There is absolutely no Scripture to support the idea (common everywhere) that Christ rules the local church through *one pas-*

tor. If the doctrine of "the pastor" is right, why can no Scripture be ushered forth to support it?

3. "An orderly church," says Mr. Owen, "needs one overseer, one shepherd, one pastor." That sounds nice, and is everywhere accepted as true, but where is this notion taught in the NT?

Everywhere one turns in the NT—the church [singular]—has shepherds [plural]. There is no example in the NT of an orderly church having *one* overseer. The orderly church in Philippi consisted of "saints, bishops and deacons" (Phil. 1:1). James said that if one was sick, "let him call for the elders [plural] of the church [singular]" (James 5:14). Paul "called the elders [plural] of the church [singular]" at Ephesus (Acts 20:17). After their first missionary journey, Paul and Barnabas saw "elders [plural] in every church [singular]" set apart (Acts 14:23). Paul left Titus in Crete to "set in order the things that are lacking, and ordain elders [plural] in every city [singular]" (Titus 1:5).

Thus, while Mr. Owen asserts that an "orderly" church needs *one* overseer, the fact is that a church without elders [plural] is designated as "lacking."

W.B. Johnson, the first President of the Southern Baptist Convention (1845), wrote in 1846:

> In a review of these Scriptures we have these points clearly made out:
>
> 1. That over each church of Christ in the Apostolic age, a plurality of elders was ordained, who were designated by the terms *elder, bishop, overseer, pastor,* with authority in the government of the flock.
>
> 2. That this authority involved no *legislative* power or right, but that it was *ministerial* and *executive* only, and that, in its exercise, the rulers were not to lord it over God's heritage, but as examples to lead the flock to the performance of duty....

3. That these rulers were all equal in rank and authority, no one having a pre-eminence over the rest.
This satisfactorily appears from the fact that the
same qualifications were required of all. So that
though some labored in word and doctrine, and
others did not, the distinction between them was
not in rank, but in the character of their service....

4. That the members of the flock were required to follow, *imitate*, the faith of their rulers, in due consideration of the end of their conversation, Jesus
Christ, the same yesterday, and today, and forever....

It is worthy of particular attention, that each church
had a plurality of elders, and although there was a difference in their respective departments of service, there
was a perfect equality of rank among them ("The Gospel Developed Through the Government and Order of
the Churches of Jesus Christ," reprinted in *Baptist Reformation Review*, 4:2-3, Summer/Autumn, 1975, pp.
29-30).

Southern Baptists as a whole—along with the bulk of
Evangelicals—have departed from W.B. Johnson's summary of
NT teaching on this matter.

4. "Allow this old veteran," Mr. Owen continues, "to observe
that chaos easily develops where no one is in charge. If the
church is to be one flock, it needs one shepherd. Let him be
the first among equals." The early churches had plural oversight,
and they apparently did very well. Mr. Owen wrongly equates
"order" with the rule of one man. But "chaos" was avoided in
the NT churches through plural eldership.

The flock indeed is *one* because it is in union with its Shepherd,
Christ. Mr. Owen sees order maintained through *one man*; the
NT sees the Great Shepherd as caring for His churches (*cf.* Rev.
1:18-20; 2:2,11, et al.).

As most of you know, it rarely works out that "the pastor" is "first among equals." He is too often the first above subordinates. The very nature of the pastor's office gives leadership to one person that is meant to be shared by a plurality of persons (*cf.* Heb. 13:17).

5. Mr. Owen believes that "the pastor" must "not abdicate his Biblically-based assignment to oversee the church." *There is no Biblical mandate anywhere for one man to oversee a local church.* The charges Paul gave regarding oversight were directed to the group of pastors from the Ephesian church, not to one person (*cf.* Acts 20:17-38).

6. Mr. Owen states that "wise church members will encourage" the advisability of one person overseeing the church. It seems to me that wise Christians, and those who fill the niche of "the pastor" must *challenge*, not continue this notion. If "the pastor" idea cannot be substantiated from the pages of the NT, why should we continue it? Should we not rather orient ourselves around the goal of plural oversight?

7. Mr. Owen touches on something that I believe is significant. He says, "from the beginning the church was a fellowship of people…. The church itself was a "*Ho Koinonia*" [the fellowship]." I am convinced that *before* the plurality of elders will make sense to believers, they must *first* see that *they have responsibilities as priests. A functioning eldership* is simply an extension of a *functioning priesthood of believers.*

For example, all Christians are encouraged to "admonish one another" (*cf.* Rom. 15:14; 1 Thess. 5:11, 14). But elders have the specific responsibility—because of their proven maturity—to "admonish" the flock (*cf.* 1 Thess. 5:12).

All Christians are to watch over one another in a caring, loving way (*cf.* Heb. 3:13; 10:24-25). But elders have a specific responsibility, for they must give account to God of their watch over the flock (*cf.* Heb. 13:17). The First London Baptist Confession (1646) put it like this:

> Christ, for the keeping of this church in holy and or- derly communion, places some special men over the church; who by their office, are to govern, oversee, visit, watch; so likewise, for the better keeping thereof, in all places by the members, He has given authority, and laid duty upon all to watch over one another (*cf.* Article 44).

Our churches are so used to having one person, or a few peo- ple, do everything, that the idea of *every member* having some- thing necessary to contribute (*cf.* Eph. 4:16) is foreign to our practice. We have acted as though the body is one part instead of many parts (*cf.* 1 Cor. 12:14). *Priests are to function, and elders are to watch over and equip the priesthood* (*cf.* 1 Peter 2:5; Eph. 4:11,12).

There is no evidence anywhere in the NT for the primacy of one person's gifts. There is evidence 58 times in the NT for the importance of *mutual care and multiple gifts*: "love one another...admonish one another...edify one another...com- fort one another...forgive one another...give to one another... pray for one another." Why are our churches marked by obvi- ous emphasis on "the pastor," but very little—if any—concern for the cultivation of *mutual relationships? We have exalted that for which there is no evidence, and neglected that for which there is abundant evidence.* We are used to pawning off *our* respon- sibilities on someone else. We want the church to minister *to us*, but we think very little as to how we can minister to the needs of others.

Our practices focus on "the pastor," and the ministry of the saints one to another is virtually non-existent. Are not our pri- orities mixed up? Robert Girard captures the spirit of what I am getting at by saying:

> Suburban America is a society of fences and private tract homes into which each family retreats, locks the door, pulls the drapes, and sits down to watch television for

the next forty years, hoping no one interrupts. The "New Society" (the kingdom community), Christ's NT dream of the church contradicts and challenges this pattern.... Too long the church has just gone along with the world's way of not relating to one another. The church has decided not to disturb the status quo for fear of offending people who want to keep their privacy and loneliness. But we have been called to reject that life-style—to move into Christ's New Society. To be a house for priests! A society of ministers! A family of people who really care for each other!

When the church gathers, as the NT tells it, it is the happy gathering of a loving family at the supper table. Its ministry when gathered is described in Scripture like a smorgasbord, a pot-luck supper, what the church used to call a 'love feast' or 'agape.' It is not one expert cook preparing one dish for everyone. It is each person bringing to the supper table what he or she has prepared – the thing each does best...All share, all eat, all are fed (*Brethren Hang Together*, pp. 132-133).

I have shared my heart with you in the fear of God. I have forthrightly challenged a prevailing viewpoint. Tradition says loudly: "an orderly church needs one overseer, one shepherd, one pastor." The NT repeatedly shows that each church had a *plurality of pastors*. Am I right or wrong? Can *you* demonstrate from Scripture that Mr. Owen's one-pastor position is really the correct view? By stating a contrary position, I have become vulnerable. I am open to correction from God's Word.

Jesus said some fearful words to the Pharisees that I believe apply to us in this regard:

"This people honors me with their lips, but their heart is far away from me. But in vain do they worship me, teaching as doctrines human precepts. Neglecting the commandment of God, you hold to human traditions." He was also saying to them, "You neatly set aside the commandment of God in order to keep your tradition" (Mark 7:6-9).

The heart far from God is connected here to disobedience of God's Word. If we keep "the pastor" tradition in order to avoid our duties as priests, and to avoid obedience to Christ's order for the churches, we become no better than a pack of Pharisees. Jesus also said, "Why do you call me, Lord, Lord, and do not the things that I say?" (Luke 6:46). We rightly claim Jesus as Lord; but will we evidence concern for specific obedience—for *change*—to God's Word? Or will we just go on in our vain (and harmful) traditions? Samuel told Saul that God was not interested in sacrifice without obedience: "Has the Lord as much delight in burnt offering and sacrifices as in obeying the voice of the Lord? Behold, to obey is better than sacrifice, and to heed than the fat of rams" (1 Sam. 15:22).

Moses was admonished concerning the construction of the Tabernacle: "See, he says, that you make all things according to the pattern showed to you in the mount" (Heb. 8:5). Likewise, in the life of Christ's churches, we are not at liberty to construct as we please. We are given general principles as to "how to behave" in the churches—a "pattern" has been given to us in the NT (1 Tim. 3:15). If the "pattern" of the *functioning priesthood of all believers* is clearly revealed, should we not get the lead out and practice the truth? What holds us back from obedience?

Mr. Owen says that "the fellowship was to have a holy place to meet." Oops! There are no holy places under the new covenant. Rather, there is a holy *people*. And these people are all baptized by one Spirit into *one* body (*cf.* 1 Cor. 12:13). Their commitment to Christ brings with it a commitment to those in Christ's body. It seems to me that this is where the rub comes: *we are hesitant to pursue the implications of what it means to "love one another" sacrificially.* We like a *private* salvation that entails no extension of ourselves to others. "The pastor" is a convenient way to pass off our duties to one saint. As James said, "Brethren, these things ought not to be" (3:10).

I submit these things to you as one concerned for the truth of Christ. I submit these things to your judgment as you search the Scriptures to see what is so (*cf.* Acts 17:11). I ask us to proceed in obedience to these perspectives, or show cause from Scripture why we shouldn't.

The letters to the seven churches in Revelation 2 & 3 indicate that Christ is not indifferent as to what goes on in His churches. He cares, and in areas of disobedience He calls the church to repentance (*cf.* Rev. 2:5, 16; 3:3). If there is indifference, coldness, and flagrant disregard for Christ's will, the Head of the churches promises to remove the candlestick from the local assembly (*cf.* Rev. 2:5).

Do these considerations move your heart? Then let us obey Christ because we love Him, in response to the great love He manifested by laying down His life for us (*cf.* John 14:15; 1 John 3:16; 4:10-11).

— Jon Zens

THE "CLERGY/LAITY" DISTINCTION:

HELP OR HINDRANCE TO THE BODY OF CHRIST?

(This article originally appeared in Searching Together, *23:4, Winter, 1995)*

In February 1996, several well-known Christian leaders hosted a "Clergy Conference" in Atlanta. These kinds of events, though undoubtedly well intended, nevertheless serve to perpetuate what I believe to be an unhealthy division of God's people into two classes: the "clergy" and the "laity"—a distinction that is totally without biblical justification. The letter I sent to the sponsors of this Atlanta conference is reproduced below.

To: The sponsors of the Atlanta "Clergy Conference"

Re: Undermining the authority of God's Word by your promotion of the unscriptural "Clergy/Laity" distinction:

In several weeks you will be having a "Clergy Conference" in Atlanta. I know you are well meaning in your desire to support and affirm the "clergy." However, in assuming this category of the "ordained," you are overlooking a more basic and pressing question that must be addressed: "Does the New Testament teach that there is a separate caste of church leaders designated as 'clergy' who are over the 'laity'?" It does not. I have prepared a paper on this question that is enclosed for you to ponder.

By gathering "clergymen" together you are just assenting to the status quo and, in effect, putting band-aids on it. What really needs to be done is to hold a conference where the NT's teaching on leadership is unfolded. If this were done, of course, then the tra-

ditional "clergy/laity" practice would have to be jet-
tisoned in favor of the NT patterns.

Looking at the big picture, you are really doing harm
to the very class of persons you are trying to help. By
not challenging the "clergy" system, which has brought
untold hurt to those within its pale, you end up giving
pep-talks and encouragement to people who are functioning in an office Christ has nowhere revealed in His
Word. You admit in *Men of Action* (November, 1995,
p. 4), "Pastors are worn out, discouraged, and in need
of affirmation. In fact, poll after poll reveals that most
pastors are battling isolation, depression, and loneliness. They are so beaten up by the ministry..." Actually,
the situation among the "clergy" is much worse than
this brief statement. But should this be surprising when
people are forced to fill a job description found nowhere in the NT? The most Christ-honoring and caring
thing you could do is to tell the 70,000 men that come
to Atlanta to stop being "clergy," because God's Word
teaches nothing about "clergy" —except that *all believers are clergy, they are the inheritance (kleros) of the Lord.*

I guess I have to honestly wonder: Do you leaders
care at all that the NT is, in fact, against the "clergy"
system? Are you concerned that the "clergy" system, as
James D. G. Dunn points out, does more to undermine
the canonical authority of the NT than other heresies?
You claim that God's Word must be our authority in all
matters of faith and practice. But you undermine and
nullify this confession by promoting a "clergy" system
that is damaging the lives of pastors and their families
every moment. By assuming that the "clergy" category is correct, your conference actually is perpetuating
an unbiblical system that is to the detriment of those
who attend. Does this concern you? Is your conscience
pricked because you are promoting and cultivating that
which the NT is against?

I do not think that I am beating in the air, or making a mountain out of a molehill. There is substance to my concerns. Do you care enough to give real answers to your constituents, or are you satisfied to go on encouraging a human tradition that has deeply wounded untold thousands of people?

Thank you for considering my thoughts and article.

— Jon

My letter to the sponsors of the recent "Clergy Conference" in Atlanta reflects my deep concern over the biblically unjustified practice of dividing God's people into two classes—pulpiteers and pew-sitters. It is a pattern that certainly reflects the hierarchical patterns of the world, but which does not square with NT teaching.

This baseless "clergy/laity" distinction has become such an assumed given that it permeates nearly all of our evangelical literature. The excerpts and snippets provided at the end of this article have been gleaned from magazines, books, catalogues and advertisements and are typical of the extent to which the "clergy/laity" division has become a part of our evangelical language and environment.

The following material has been adapted from the article I submitted with my letter to the conference sponsors. I have no desire to stir up unnecessary dissension, but I believe that if the Church is to attain her full potential as the visible body of Christ, she must divest herself of such unscriptural hierarchical structures and return to her intended "one-another" relationships and ministries.

Before we examine the historical and biblical evidence, consider the following three examples of the kind of teaching that has influenced this "clergy/laity" thinking:

1. "On this office [of Pastor] and the discharge of it He has laid the whole weight of the order, rule, and edification of His Church."[1]

2. "[The Pastor] is like the cerebellum, the center for communicating messages, coordinating functions, and conducting responses between the head and body.... The
pastor is not only the authoritative communicator of the
truth from the Head to the body, but he is also the accurate communicator of the needs from the Body to the
Head."[2]

3. "[Pastor Hamman] likened the total church to an army.
'The army has only one Commander-in-Chief, Jesus
Christ. The local church is like a company with one company commander, the pastor, who gets his orders from
the Commander-in-Chief. The company commander has
lieutenants and sergeants under him for consultation and
implementation, but the final responsibility for decisions
is that of the company commander, and he must answer
to the Commander-in-Chief'... The Pastor has the power
in a growing church.... The pastor of a growing church
may appear to outsiders as a dictator, but to the people of
the church, his decisions are their decisions."[3]

A recent ad in an evangelical magazine had the heading, "Not
Every Question Gets Answered On Sunday Morning." The
truth is that probably no one's questions are answered because
no inquiries are allowed. The pulpit monologue precludes dialogue. The pulpit can only be occupied by certain people: the
"clergy." The rest—the "laity"—sit in pews. In this dichotomy
you have the essence of our religion —Catholic, Protestant, or
otherwise —in a nutshell: the "clergy" are paid to give and the
"laymen" pay in order to receive. This distinction permeates our
religious vocabulary, and unfortunately captures the heart of our
practice: we pay the "clergy" to do the necessary religious activities. It is wearying to hear refrains like these repeated in so many
evangelical advertisements: "Finally, a book that both pastors
and laymen can understand"..."this video is equally profitable
for clergy and laity."

While the "clergy/laity" distinction is embedded and assumed in religious circles, it cannot be found in the NT. It reared up its ugly head in the third century, long after Christ's apostles died. We should be pointedly reminded of the utter deceitfulness of sin when we realize how deeply such an unscriptural and damaging concept has taken root in visible Christianity.

The NT teaches leadership among the people of God, but not in a way that leads to the "clergy/laity" conclusion. The root words from which we derive the English words "clergy" and "laity" are found in the NT, but our usage of "clergy/laity" is far removed from the NT concepts.

Clergy...

The English word "clergy" is related to the Greek word "*kleros.*" It means "a lot or inheritance." For example, in 1 Peter 5:3 the elders are exhorted not to lord it over "the lots" (Greek: *ton kleron*), which refers to the entire flock of God's people. Nowhere in the NT is any form of "*kleros*" used to designate a separate class of "ordained" leaders. Instead, it refers to the "inheritance" (Greek: *klerou*) laid up for all the saints (*cf.* Col. 1:12; Acts 26:18). The saints as a collective whole are conceived of in the NT as God's "inheritance." We have utterly perverted and turned upside-down the NT teaching by using the term "clergy" to refer to a special elite group of church leaders.

Laity...

This English word is related to the Greek word "*laos*," which means "people." The Greek word "*laikos*," which means "laity," is not found in the NT. All in the body of Christ, whether "saints, bishops, or deacons" (Phil. 1:1), are the "people" (*laos*) of God. "People of God" is a title of honor bestowed upon all who believe in the Lord Jesus Christ (*cf.* 2 Cor. 6:16; 1 Peter 2:9-10).

It was not until the third century that "clergy" was employed to designate a limited number of persons who functioned in the

Christian assemblies. One of the worst outcomes of the "clergy" doctrine was that it communicated the notion that without the "clergy" present there simply was no church. Baptism, the Lord's Supper, and many other church practices, could not happen unless "clergy" were present. This idea persists to our day even in the workplace, as James D. G. Dunn notes, when "some of the early statements regarding industrial chaplaincies... seemed to imply that the church was not present in industry unless and until an ordained clergyman became involved on the factory floor."[4]

Because the NT knows nothing of "clergy," the fact that a separate caste of the "ordained" permeated our vocabulary and practice illustrates rather forcefully that we do not yet take the NT very seriously. The "clergy" practice is a heresy that must be renounced. It strikes at the heart of the priesthood of all believers that Jesus purchased on the cross. It contradicts the shape Jesus' kingdom was to take when He said, "You are all brothers and sisters." Since it is a human tradition, it nullifies the Word of God (cf. Mark 7:13). Dunn sees the emergence of "clergy" as a very negative historical fact:

> When Clement resorted once again to the distinction between "priest" and "laity" (cf. 1 Clem. 40:5), he was pointing down a road, which would fundamentally compromise, if not make a mere cipher of, a very basic element in earliest Christianity's self-understanding... It is the apparent disregard for something quite so fundamental by subsequent Christian history that does more to undermine the canonical authority of the NT than most heresies... The major authority acknowledged by all Christians [the NT] has been effectively discounted and ignored.[5]

Every Christian tradition has its insights and blind spots. But the "clergy" system is practiced across the board and is thus a universal blind spot. Seminaries and Bible Schools have multiplied to produce people for the "clergy" profession; ministerial conferences abound to supply support and encouragement that the "laity" cannot give; magazines are published to provide ministerial tips; pastoral search committees must be formed every time a minister moves on; clergy counseling must be provided for those who burn out and have nervous breakdowns; etc., etc. A whole intricate system is in place to perpetuate and preserve a role, which the NT knows nothing about.

Like it or not, this "clergy" role ends up requiring a virtual omni-competence from those behind the pulpit. "Clergy" are paid to perform whatever is necessary to keep the religious machinery going, and the expectations are very high for those who wear the many coats this profession demands.

The deadly problem with this unscriptural system is that it eats up those within its pale. Burnout, depression, and suicide are very high among the "clergy." Is it any wonder such repeated tragedies occur in light of what is expected of one person? Christ never intended anyone to fill such an ecclesiastical role. In light of Paul's remark in 1 Corinthians 12:14 that "the body is not one part but many," we should be able to discern that the "clergy" position is neither healthy for those in it, nor is it beneficial for the body of Christ.

Scholars have debated the propriety of ordaining women as "clergy." However, a larger, more fundamental question has been passed over in the process: should anyone, male or female, be ordained as "clergy," since the Bible does not know of such an office?[6]

The terms "Reformation" and "Renewal" are buzzwords in religious publications. Sadly, most periodicals of this sort assume that the "clergy" system is sacrosanct, thereby reinforcing its stronghold in contemporary churches. I submit that to seek the renewal of the "laity" while perpetuating the "clergy" system is like mixing oil and water. Deep renewal (a healthy body) will come only as every member contributes his/her gifts and graces, which includes a leadership that practices the servant model revealed by Jesus in Mark 10:42-45. The "clergy" system stands as a monumental obstacle to genuine reformation and renewal.

The church must jettison this system in order for the Word of God to have free course.

If those who function as "clergy" come to the conviction that this role originates from unscriptural traditions and not from NT patterns, I suggest eight practical steps that must be taken:

1. Stop using "Pastor," "Reverend," and other religious titles in connection with your names (and encourage others to cease using language that reflects the "clergy/laity" distinction).

2. Renounce your "clergy" status and see yourself as part of the "*laos*" of God, which has manifestations of the Spirit, along with everyone else, for the good of the body (*cf.* 1 Cor. 12:7). This practically means that you should no longer view yourself as the leader or "head" of the church. You are one member among many. Jesus is the head. That must be more than religious rhetoric.

3. Teach the body that your "clergy" roles and all the expectations that go with them are based on human traditions and not the gospel.

4. Instruct the brethren that all aspects of caring for one another rest with the body, not on some spiritual elite.

5. Begin a new methodology of truth seeking and truth-speaking. Instead of the "clergy" spoon-feeding the "laity," study important issues together from the Word with a view to finding Christ's will and acting upon it.

6. Adopt a teaching style where dialogue occurs and questions/insight from others are encouraged. Allow and encourage other members of the body to teach, preach, and share. This isn't your exclusive domain.

7. As the body makes concrete changes in the way "church" is done the emphasis shifts from dependency on one person to edifying, multiple participation. I recommend

that you invite someone who has experience living in and planting organic churches to help bring you along in the process.

8. Your financial support as a clergy person is admittedly a difficult issue, but needs to be creatively evaluated. The traditional view that it is necessary to pay the "clergy" to preach, visit parishioners, do various administrative duties, etc., is without NT foundation. As long as "clergy" are paid to do religious duties why should the body develop its "one-another" ministries? Paul testified to the elders at Ephesus: "I coveted no one's silver, gold, or costly garments. You yourselves know personally that these hands ministered to my own needs and those of others with me. In everything I have pointed out to you that, by working in this way diligently, we ought to support the weak, being mindful of Jesus' words, 'It is more blessed to give than to receive'" (Acts 20: 33-35). As ministry becomes increasingly shared in the body, it takes the load off one person and frees the congregation to evaluate how its financial resources can be maximized for edification and meeting people's needs.[7]

Obviously, the "clergy" system has become a mammoth institution. When you touch this nerve the whole body quivers. This long-standing system will not disappear overnight. Not every "clergy" person takes the NT seriously, but those who do need to lead the way by personal example to a paradigm shift, which will better reflect the NT revelation of church life. People who withdraw from the traditional "clergy" model out of faithfulness to Christ will have a heavy price to pay. Nevertheless, the question still remains: Is our confession that the NT is *sufficient* for faith and practice a reality or a sham? If we are serious about following Christ, how can we remain party to perpetuating a "clergy" system, which contradicts the very essence of the ecclesia our Savior purposed to build? When is enough, enough?

There are at least 58 commands in the NT unfolding our "one-another" responsibilities, and zero in the NT about "the pastor" being the cerebellum...the one company commander in the local church...the one who has the power...upon whose shoulders rests the whole weight of the order, rule, and edification of His church. When are we going to wake up and realize that the evil one has tricked us into squandering resources for a "clergy" system that is unknown in, and opposed to, the NT? This has thereby diverted us from spending ourselves for all the implications of loving one another, for which there is abundant NT warrant. Larry Crabb summarizes a crucial goal that believers should have in their life together:

> Change takes place when truth is presented in relationships. Perhaps a relationship of deep regard and empathetic concern is the context for change, creating an atmosphere in which the truth of God can be heard non-defensively and thus penetrate more deeply... To be healthy, a church must present truth in the context of encouraging relationships.[8]

The reality in local church life is that nothing hinders the fostering and cultivating of encouraging relationships more than the "clergy/laity" distinction. It stands as a huge roadblock to the very atmosphere we desperately need in our assemblies. The time has come for each of us to personally take the responsibility to live a life that refuses to knuckle under the stifling "clergy/laity" tradition, and to begin fresh new paths of obedience, where the body of Christ functions as vital parts contributing to the growth of the whole (cf. Eph. 4:11-16).

ENDNOTES:

1. John Owen, *True Nature of a Gospel Church*, abridged edition, p. 55.

2. David L. McKenna, "The Ministry's Gordian Knot," *Leadership*, Winter, 1980, pp. 30-31.

3. C. Peter Wagner, *Your Church Can Grow*, Regal 1976, pp. 66-67.

4. James D.G. Dunn "Priesthood, Eucharist, and Ordination," *New Testament Theology in Dialogue*, Westminster Press, 1987 p. 127.

5. Ibid., pp. 127-129.

6. *Cf.* Marjorie Warkentin, *Ordination: A Biblical-Historical View*, Eerdmans, 1982, 202 pages.

7. Here are some thoughts for institutional pastors who are feeling the tug to pursue Christ organically. Check out http://housechurchresource.org/expastors/ and the "Survival Guide" in that context. Read *Finding Organic Church* by Frank Viola. It was written for people in your situation. Feel free to contact me at jzens@searchingtogether.org with any further questions.

8. *Encouragement: The Key To Caring*, Zondervan, 1984, pp. 84, 91.

HERE ARE A NUMBER OF TYPICAL EVERY-DAY ALLUSIONS TO "CLERGY/LAITY" IN OUR CHRISTIANESE:

» "No Christian, whether minister or lay member can build on any ..."

» "The clergy and laymen who sided with Hitler gained 70 ..."

» "A guide to show how churches can bridge the communications gap between pastor and congregation ..."

» "This journal was created with input from more than 25 pastors and lay persons ..."

» "In-depth look at the pastor's role as a team member working with lay persons ..."

» "Dialogue between a voice from the pew and a voice from the seminary —between laity and clergy. Written in every-day language ..."

» "Lay person's Introduction to the Old Testament ..."

» "Speaking to both pastors and lay persons, Dr. Proctor offers spirit-enriching ..."

» "I was a pastor who needed help. Unfortunately, my church couldn't offer any direction ..."

» "Emphasizing the Pastor's role as equipper of the laity, Myrlene Hamilton recognizes ..."

» "A Reforming Church: Gift and Task—a conference for Pastors and Lay people..."

» "While some lay persons and pastors still are very skeptical about the recovery ..."

» "Today American Baptist clergy called to chaplaincy and pastoral counseling labor in organ transplant ..."

» "There laity and clergy, denominational leaders and missionaries have grappled with issues ..."

» "We hope clergy will encourage a number of small lay led
groups, in each congregation ..."

» "Some 300 persons —pastors and laity—attended this conference ..."

» "A total of 46 lay persons participated in the yearly summer
sessions ..."

» "Yes, I will be able to attend: __ Myself and spouse __
Layman and wife."

» "Providing a place and time for fellowship, support and col-
legiality for the clergy of our area ..."

» "I simply wanted to be better prepared to defend and promote them as a good lay person should. I thought a year or
two of Bible school would stay with me the rest of my life."

» "DAKOTA IS TEMPORARILY WITHOUT PASTORAL
SERVICES: We regret to announce the resignation of Elder
Jerry Morgan from the Alfred, North Dakota church. This
resignation took place October First. Brother Morgan took
a pastorate in the Oklahoma City area. We are very disappointed to see him leave the district, but do wish him well
in his new pastorate..."

» "Clergy Sexual Abuse: Wives who were victims of domestic
violence in the parsonage continue to call attention to the
corruption, which is eating away all credibility in the community and the profession..."

» "A Handbook for Clergy and Church Members..."

» "Give Your Pastor A Boost Next Month."

» "Did you know that October 1994 has been designated 'Clergy Appreciation Month'? Focus on the Family, in conjunction with the National Day of Prayer, Promise Keepers..."

» "Under His Wings Ministries, Inc. and a host of denominations, is encouraging local congregations to honor their clergy and family in a special way..."

» "Nor is it polite to put a guest on the spot by asking him or her to say grace at your table. The exception is a guest who is a member of the clergy: this is a rare exception to the rule against asking guests to do socially in your home what they do professionally outside it..."

» "While much has been said and written about equipping the laity, churches during this century have become more and more dependent upon leadership from the clergy..."

» "P.S. - Don't tell Pastor - it's a surprise!"

» "Clergy Getaways..."

» "Clergy: Persons who have received tonsure or Holy Orders; those elevated to a higher rank than the laity and given a special duty in the divine service or in administering to the Church. Sometimes the use of the word includes all religious, even sisters and lay brothers..."

» "But in the institutionalized church, and especially in large congregations, a minority of members are actively engaged in the church's business while the remainder only make up the audience. Among the so-called laity there are only a few functions possible, such as teaching Sunday School, participating in prayer meetings, and helping raise money. The really significant religious functions are matters for the clergy or the ministers..." (Floyd Mackler)

Letter from Dan in Romania:

Thanks for writing back, Jon

I was waiting for a response and I really appreciate your words. I read your email and also the "The Pastor" article. The ideas of Frank Owen are present in the mentality of the Baptist church in Romania.

I will tell you something about my story. In the seminary I began to see many things about the position of the pastor, that they were wrong. But one situation opened my eyes more clearly. The pastor from my local town where I grew up considered his position threatened by me during my studies at the seminary. At the beginning he asked me to help the youth ministry because my town is near Bucharest. So I did. In my last year at the seminary, because of some problems, the pastor said to the church that he desired to leave and he resigned. The next day I went to him and I asked him about this decision. He said to me that the Lord guided him in that decision. After 2 weeks he convoked the church and he said to the people that he changed his mind, and that others actually wanted his resignation. They were two different stories. So I told that to him in the church and he interpreted my intervention to mean that I wanted his position. And God knows that I didn't want that!

After that, he made many problems for me at the seminary, and I was close to losing my studies. I was called to the pastors' meeting in Bucharest to justify what I said in the church about the pastor. They put me under discipline because I wasn't on the pastor's side, even though he lied and spread false things about me. They told to me that I am a rebel against the pastor and the church. All these things affected me, and I thought that it was better for me if I didn't say anything. But, I started to see more the errors of the religious system.

After that I finally finished at the seminary, I was valedictorian, and a church (the church where I live now) proposed for me to be the youth leader. After I get married, the senior pastor wants to ordain me. But our views are very different, because he is a very much a "system guy." After your reply I had a very strong discussion with him. He said to me that I must call him "brother pastor" not " brother," because he is the senior pastor and the church must know that there is a pastor. I was very surprised in a negative way, and I told him that Jesus said in Matthew 23 not to use religious titles. He did not take this well, and it put a distance between us. He has many good qualities, but he wants to be in charge. He said to me that he is the senior pastor and that he will give the direction of the church, not me, and I have to be very conscious of that. These things assure me more that I am not the right guy for this kind of job or position. I can't deny my beliefs. On the other hand, it will be difficult for me to leave because I don't have another profession, and I want to get married next year, and in Romania it is so hard now to find a job. I am not sure what to do, but soon I will take a decision. I cannot continue in the "system."

Thanks again,
Dan

(The whole reply can be seen at www.paganchristianity.org/zens.htm)

One brother in the South recently read Dr. Witherington's review and my full reply, and commented—"I really appreciated your thoughts and insights, but more importantly, your gracious and Christ-exalting attitude and humility. Your words and demeanor offer a striking example for all of us to follow. I saw you refer to your age on Facebook, 66, I believe. I am 33. Obviously, a different generation. I have longed for those in the generation before me to set this type of example to follow. I know I don't know you personally, but I look forward to learning from you and your experience through your articles and books. Perhaps one day, we shall meet face to face."

Professor Witherington, for years I have deeply appreciated your insightful studies, especially concerning the cultural settings of Jesus, Paul, the church and women. You have truly opened some crucial gates for better understanding and applying the NT documents.

Your opening comments about *Pagan Christianity* [*PC*] were not very satisfying to me. I've been wrestling with "church" issues for thirty years, and it would be my conclusion that *PC* accurately reflects the basic conclusions—even virtual consensus—of a wide range of NT theologians and church historians.

For example, it would appear that James D.G. Dunn's summary remarks capture the essence of *PC*'s heartbeat:

> Increasing institutionalism is the clearest mark of early
> Catholicism —when church becomes increasingly iden-
> tified with institution, when authority becomes increas-
> ingly coterminous with office, when a basic distinction

between clergy and laity becomes increasingly self-ev-
ident, when grace becomes increasingly narrowed to
well-defined ritual acts. We saw above that such features
were absent from first generation Christianity, though
in the second generation the picture was beginning to
change (*Unity & Diversity in the New Testament,* Westminster Press, 1977, p. 351).

You rightly note, "The question is which traditions comport
with Biblical tradition and which do not." I believe that *PC*
has done an admirable job of trying to sort out the contours
of organic life reflected in the NT from the subsequent trap-
pings that sapped the life out of the church. There is great liberty under the New Covenant. But surely we are not free to
do "church" in any way we please. Surely not everything that
calls itself "church" is really *ekklesia*. Aren't we supposed to pay
attention to the "apostolic traditions"? Isn't the acid test of any
church form whether or not it fosters and cultivates NT values?
Isn't it safe to say that the great majority of post-apostolic traditions only served to move the church away from NT simplicity?

Your statement that "Everyone agrees that the church is a
living thing and organism, not an organization," fails to reckon
with the fact that history is replete with examples where insti-
tutionalization kills life. The truth is that many forms of church
are out of sync with the DNA of the *ekklesia*. Many environments are hostile to organic life. *PC* rightly points out that there
is good reason to question if the inherited ways of doing church
are conducive to promoting the growth of living forms.

"Christians continued to meet with Jews in synagogues." I
see no evidence in the NT that Christian gatherings were held in
synagogues. The times Paul and a few others visited synagogues
was not to have a gospel-based gathering, but to proclaim Christ
from the OT evangelistically.

"There were plenty of tribal religions in the Ancient Near
East that could not afford and did not have Temples, or priests."
The truth is, however, that the overwhelmingly vast majority
of religions have been marked by the presence of, as John H.

Yoder called him/her, "the religious specialist." Yoder rightly observes:

> There are few more reliable constants running through all human society than the special place every human community makes for the professional religionist.... in every case he disposes a unique quality, which he usually possesses for life, which alone qualifies him for his function, and beside, which the mass of men are identifiable negatively as "laymen," i.e., non-bearers of this special quality.... One person per place is enough to do what he needs to do.... The clergyman mediates between the common life and the realm of the "invisible" or the "spiritual".... No one balks at what his services cost ("The Fullness of Christ," reprinted in *Searching Together*, 11:3, 1982, pp. 4-7).

The whole "clergy" tradition has no basis in the NT, and is one of the most enormous obstacles to the Body of Christ functioning as it should. Roman Catholic William Bausch makes these astute observations:

> Our survey has shown us that no cultic priesthood is to be found in the New Testament. Yet we wound up importing Old Testament Levitical forms and imposing them on Christian ministry.... Nevertheless in practice there is no denying that there has historically been a gathering into one person and his office what were formerly the gifts of many.... [This practice] goes astray, of course, when it translates to mean that only ordination gives competence, authority, and the right of professional governance. It goes further astray when eventually all jurisdictional and administrative powers in the church come to be seen as an extension of the sacramental powers conferred at ordination. In short, there is a movement here away from the more pristine collaborative and mutual ministries of the New Testament (*Traditions,*

Tensions, Transitions in Ministry, Twenty-Third Publications, 1982, pp. 54, 30).

You seem to totally miss the point when you say, "I was also surprised by the bold claim that there were no sacred persons." Of course, the authors affirm that all of God's people are "holy ones." What was meant is that in Christ's kingdom there are no "holy persons," in the sense of the "religious expert" Yoder described above, who is a notch above the "lay" people because of some special ceremony, often called "ordination."

The "recognition" of functions portrayed in the NT is a very far cry from the "ordination" to office that developed in post-apostolic times (*cf.* Marjorie Warkentin, *Ordination: A Biblical-Historical View*, Eerdmans, 1980). You seem to merge the two together as if they are organically connected.

You suggest that, "The ecclesial structure of the NT church was hierarchical." It would seem that Jesus' corrective remarks to the Twelve ruled out such a model of leadership – "not so among you." There are many scholars who would differ with your conclusion. One example among many would be Herbert Haag, a Roman Catholic himself, whose examination of the evidence led him to assert:

> In the Catholic Church there are two classes, clergy and laity.... This structure does not correspond to what Jesus did and taught. Consequently it has not had a good effect in the history of the Church.... Among his disciples Jesus did not want any distinction of class or rank.... In contradiction to this instruction of Jesus, a "hierarchy," a "sacred authority," was nevertheless formed in the third century (*Upstairs, Downstairs: Did Jesus Want a Two-Class Church?*, Crossroad, 1997, p. 109).

You suggest that the NT views the Lord's Supper as a "sacrament," but I do not think this is accurate. As *PC* points out, the Lord's Supper, as instituted by Jesus and practiced in the early church, was a *meal together*. Leonard Verduin gave a number of reasons why the transformation of a meal into a post-apostolic "sacrament" was retrogressive and connected to alien pagan influences (cf. *The Reformers & Their Stepchildren*, Eerdmans, 1964, pp. 137-142). As Vernard Eller noted, "the whole style of thought that goes along with the concept 'sacrament' is just plain foreign to the NT" ("The Lord's Supper is Not a Sacrament," *Searching Together*, 12:3, 1983, p. 3).

In closing, I would like to make this observation that I would think should give us pause for serious reflection. In the period when the early church blossomed incredibly with divine love and spiritual power, it had no special buildings, no clergy, and no fixed ritual (cf. Graydon Snyder, *First Corinthians: A Faith Community Commentary*, Mercer, 1992, pp. 248-249; William A. Beardslee, *First Corinthians: A Commentary for Today*, Chalice Press, 1994, pp. 136-137). When church edifices, clergy and fixed rituals became prominent, the visible church became focused on perpetuating itself and lost the simplicity of Christ. This is why I believe the information in *PC* has appeared for such a time as this, when the Body of Christ needs to recapture a NT vision regarding the "new humanity" in Christ....

Your entire review is built on a huge but false assumption that you never support. This assumption is the linchpin for your entire argument. Here is the assumption: *That the Christian meeting in the first century was a gathering for worship, i.e., a "worship service."*

This assumption cannot be substantiated anywhere from the NT. There is no place in all of Scripture that teaches that Christians are to gather for "worship." Other scholars agree. For example, in chapter 9 of his seminal work, *Paul's Idea of Community*, Dr. Robert Banks discusses Romans 12:1-2, which says that our whole life is to be worship unto the Lord. He then makes this crucial point, "since all places and times have now become the venue of worship" (cf. Rom. 12:1-2), Paul cannot speak of Christian assembly in church distinctively for this purpose."

You suggest that in 1 Corinthians 10, the word "table" *could* refer to a piece of liturgical furniture. Your words: "Could it be

that there was actually a table involved—a piece of liturgical furniture?" This is quite a stretch and an extremely thin argument
to refute the authors' point that the early church meetings were
simple and marked by open sharing centered on Jesus Christ
Himself. The fact is that the word *trapedzes* is used for an ordinary table where one eats a meal (*cf.* Matt 15:27; Mark 7:28,
Luke 22:21, etc.).

Many scholars have shown that the Lord's Supper in the first
century was taken as a full meal (*cf.* Robert Banks, I. Howard
Marshall, *et al.* See also Eric Svendsen's work, *The Table of the
Lord*). Each argue that the Lord's Supper would occur around
the same table or tables that they ate from every day. In Acts
16:34 the word *trapedzes* is used synonymously with a "meal"—
the jailer "set before them a table." To transform a common
table into a consecrated piece of religious furniture is to read
yet-to-be sacramental practices back into the NT. Therefore, it's
highly *unlikely* that the table mentioned in that text is anything
more than a table that was used to hold a meal....

To say that nowhere in the NT do we find any statement that
Jesus Christ is leading a meeting is simply false. 1 Corinthians
14 depicts a meeting where God in Christ through the Holy
Spirit is speaking through prophecy and other gifts and where
the Lord is being revealed as a result. In 1 Corinthians 14:26-33,
Paul's very words "God is not the author of confusion" suggest
that God is "authoring" [leading] the meeting, or should be....

Viola and Barna emphasize again and again that the first-
century meeting was a gathering to express Jesus Christ through
the every-member functioning of His body. It wasn't a worship
service or a bible study. While worship is included in this and
the bible is no doubt used, studying the bible or worshipping
God are not the central goals. Christ revealed and expressed is
the goal, which results in the edification of the body (*cf.* 1 Cor.
12-14; Eph. 3:9-11; 4:16).... It was stated in *Pagan Christianity*:

> In organic church life, the meetings look different ev-
> ery week. While the brothers and sisters in an organic
> church may prayerfully plan the focus of their own

meetings (for instance, they might set aside a month for the body to concentrate on Ephesians 1), they do not plan a specific order of worship. Instead, everyone is free to function, share, participate, and minister spiritually during gatherings, so the creativity expressed in them is endless. Participants do not know who will stand up and share next, nor what they will share. There might be skits; there might be poems read; there might be new songs introduced and sung; there might be exhortations, testimonies, short teachings, revelations, and prophetic words. Because everyone is involved and people contribute spontaneously, boredom is not a problem. The most meaningful meetings are generally those in which everyone participates and functions. Jesus Christ is the center of the meeting. He is glorified through the songs, the lyrics, the prayers, the ministry, and the sharing. The meeting is completely open for the Holy Spirit to reveal Christ through each member as He sees fit. In the words of 1 Corinthians 14:26, "every one of you" contributes something of Christ to the gathering. In organic church life, the corporate church meeting is an explosive outflow of what the Lord revealed of Himself to each member during the week. These features are virtually absent in the typical institutional church service.

Why must you imply that "a time together without an order of worship, without a liturgy, with a worship leader" is seriously defective? I trust you are aware that other competent scholars disagree with your assessment here.

"A time together without an order of worship, without a liturgy, without a worship leader" basically reflects what was occurring in Corinth with Paul's approbation! There is no "up-front" leadership mentioned in the 1 Corinthians 14 meeting. Paul does not put the kibosh on an open, participatory meeting. He just desires that in such a gathering all the contributions build up the whole *ekklesia* and are understood by everyone. (This argument is developed in depth in *Reimagining Church*)....

I challenged the idea that it is proper to call the Lord's Supper a "sacrament" in my response to Part One. In Part Two you use the word again and again. Calling Baptism and the Lord's Supper "sacraments" was a tragic post-NT development. I'm not the only scholar who has argued this. One of the most famous is Emil Brunner:

> Properly speaking, New Testament Christianity knows nothing of the word "sacrament," which belongs essentially to the heathen world of the Graeco-Roman empire and which unfortunately some of the Reformers unthinkingly took over from ecclesiastical tradition. For this word, and still more the overtones, which it conveys, is the starting point for those disastrous developments, which began soon to transform the community of Jesus into the Church, which is first and foremost a sacramental Church (*The Misunderstanding of the Church*, Lutterworth, 1952, pp. 72-73).

The big question for me is why so many Christians are footloose with the revelation contained in 1 Corinthians 12-14 and Hebrews 10? These are descriptions of "the meeting" of the *ekklesia*. Why do we in our praxis consign these texts to oblivion? (The exception being the part in Hebrews 10, which stays not to forsake church services!) We have elevated and set in concrete that for which there is absolutely no evidence in the NT— the pastor, the sermon and the pulpit—and in so doing lost the untold blessings of gatherings where Christ is exalted as all the parts bring forth uplifting contributions....

You put down small gatherings as "largely anthropocentric," as "looking at and to each other," and rarely resulting in "worship." But you admit that the Corinthians had 1 Corinthians 14-type meetings and the Lord's Supper in homes. Were these meetings people-centered and worship-less? I have to doubt that you would suggest that. Why were such meetings in the first century wonderful, but such gatherings in our day are suspect?...

To try to tease out of Mark 13:14 and Revelation 2 & 3 a justification for a clergy because someone "read" epistles that were sent to the believing community strains credulity. I've been in many church meetings (outside the institution) where someone read a letter to the church that was addressed to it. That didn't make them clergy. The best explanation for this is simply that those who could read in the early churches read letters to the rest of the group (illiteracy was quite high in the first century, as you know). This is another example of having to stretch the biblical material to justify "clergy"....

You write, "There is more than enough here in this book to make my hair stand on end." Part of the reason why this is happening to you is because you assume (quite wrongly, I might add) that *ekklesia* must have hierarchical leadership, religious furniture, a modern "pastor," a pulpit, and a specially dedicated religious building. As *PC* demonstrates quite compellingly, the early church had none of these things. The book then raises the question: could it be that this is because Jesus died for something very different with respect to His church?...

The authors are not arguing against biblical preaching and teaching as you assert. They are instead arguing against the modern sermon and calling into question the belief that it is the equivalent of NT preaching and teaching. As they put it themselves:

> We strongly believe in preaching, teaching, prophesying, exhorting, and all forms of sharing the Word of God. We are simply saying that the modern sermon, which we define as the *same* person (usually a clergyman) giving an oration to the *same* group of people week after week, month after month, and year after year is not only unbiblical, it is counterproductive. We want readers to look at the biblical and historical evidence for this point and decide for themselves whether or not we are correct in our analysis. In fact, research conducted

by The Barna Group has shown that sermons are generally ineffective at facilitating worship, at drawing people
closer to God, and at conveying life-changing information to those in the audience.

Despite your lengthy review, you have failed to dismantle
what is stated in *PC* regarding the entrenched traditions that
cluster around "the pastor"....

You assert: "The problem of course with home groups is that
they do not fulfill the mandate of Jesus to his disciples be 'a city
set on a hill, which cannot be hid.'" He might as well have said,
"a church hidden in a suburban home can't be found."

I guess the first-century churches that Paul established, most
of which were quite small in membership (I believe you suggest
40 in Corinth in your commentary) and all of which met in
homes, sadly didn't fulfill the mandate of Jesus. Are you suggesting that the home *ekklesias* of the first century were somehow set on a hill, but contemporary counterparts can't be? Your
comment seems to reveal a bias against a valid *ekklesia* form....

The main points of chapter three in *PC* are that the traditional way of structuring church services has dubious origins
and is patently out of sync with what is revealed in the NT. As
Ernest F. Scott noted concerning the gatherings of believers in
the early period:

> Prayer was offered, as in the Synagogue, but not in
> stated liturgical form. It was uttered freely, on the im-
> pulse of the Spirit, and was presented in the name of
> Christ, the Intercessor.... The Christian faith gave rise
> to hymns of a new character, often produced in the
> heat of the moment and almost as soon forgotten; but
> sometimes-short lyrics of real beauty were treasured and
> repeated.... Chief of all these [elements] was the obser-
> vance of the Supper.... This, indeed, was not so much
> a part of the worship as the vessel, which contained all
> the parts. The purpose of the Christian meeting was to
> hold the common meal, and to make it a memorial of

Jesus' Last Supper with the disciples.... The exercise of
the spiritual gifts was thus the characteristic element in
primitive worship. Those gifts might vary in their nature
and degree according to the capacity of each individual,
but they were bestowed on all and room was allowed in
the service for the participation of all who were present.
"When you meet together," says Paul, "each of you hath
a psalm, a teaching, a tongue, an interpretation." Every member was expected to contribute something of
his own to the common worship.... Worship in those
first days was independent of all forms (*The Nature of
the Early Church*, Charles Scribner's Sons, 1941, pp.
75,77,79,87).....

You seem to miss the point that the nexus of responsibility
to "bind and loose" is committed to the believing community,
not to "office bearers." You say, "Jesus, according to Matthew
16, founded his church on a leader named Peter. He was given
the keys to the kingdom and the power of binding and loosing."
But whatever Matt.16 teaches, that is not the whole story, is it?

In Matthew 18 we see very clearly that the "keys" to bind
and loose are in the possession of the *ekklesia*. The epistles are
addressed to bodies of believers, not to leaders. Even at Corinth
where problems and immaturity abounded, Paul addressed the
believers as possessing the spiritual resources to face and resolve
their issues. He never addressed "leaders" separately as if problem solving fell specifically upon their shoulders....

You aver that the shepherding "task is not given to everyone...in no case are all Christians called and gifted to do shepherding." In saying things like this, I think you are missing a
vital NT perspective. Without denying that some individuals
function as "shepherds," it is nevertheless the case that the task
of general oversight and pastoral care is given to everyone in the
body. If you think about it, all the characteristics of elders are
to be marks of the whole community—including instruction (*cf.*
Heb. 5:12; Rom. 15:14). The many facets of caring—including
warning the unruly, comforting the feebleminded, supporting

the weak—are to be fleshed out by the community as the whole
body functions (*cf.* 1 Thess. 5:14; see also the 58 "one another"
exhortations given to the believing community). In Galatians
6:1-2, those in the body who are walking in the Spirit are to
be involved in the restoration process when others become
ensnared in sin. In 1 John all the brethren are to "test the spirits." As John H. Yoder observes,

> The whole concern of Reformation theology was to jus-
> tify restructuring the organized church without shaking
> its foundations.... But if we were to ask whether any
> of the NT literature makes the assumptions listed—Is
> there one particular office in which there should be
> only one or a few individuals for whom it provides a
> livelihood, unique in character due to ordination, cen-
> tral to the definition of the church and the key to her
> functioning? Then the answer from the biblical material
> is a resounding "no".... The conclusion is inescapable
> that the multiplicity of ministries is not a mere *adiapho-*
> *ron*, a happenstance of only superficial significance, but
> a specific work of grace and a standard for the church....
> Let us then ask first not whether there is a clear, solid
> concept of preaching, but whether there was in the NT
> one particular preaching *office*, identifiable as distinct-
> ly as the other ministries. Neither in the most varied
> picture (Corinthians) nor in the least varied (Pastoral
> Epistles) is there one particular ministry thus defined
> ("The Fullness of Christ: Perspectives on Ministries in
> Renewal," *Concern*, No. 17, Feb. 1969).

An especially revealing passage is Hebrews 12:15 where the
verb *episkopeo* appears. The noun form of this verb, of course,
refers to "overseers," or "elders." We get our word "Episcopal"
from it. So here we have the action of "overseeing" applied to
the whole body of brothers and sisters. R.C.H. Lenski makes
these observations: "*Episcopos* is a bishop; the participle bids all
the readers to act the part of *episcopoi*, overseers, by exercising

continuous oversight of each other" (*The Interpretation of Hebrews*, p. 443). Lenski translates this as, "continuing to exercise oversight lest anyone be dropping away from the grace of God." Elders (overseers/shepherds) simply model this oversight and pastoral care for the rest of the church....

When any of Paul's churches were in crisis, Paul didn't write his corrective letters to "the pastor." He instead writes to the whole church, and he exhorts the entire church to deal with the crisis. Contrast that with today's practice. If there were a crisis brewing in the typical traditional church today, letters would be addressed to the pastor, not the congregation. In fact, a close look at the Pauline letters, as well as those of Peter, James, and John, reveals that the apostles never mention a single pastor. That there were elders/overseers/shepherds in some of them is without question, but they clearly didn't have the kind of prominence that the modern pastor is given today (for an insightful discussion on the role of first-century elders, see R. A. Campbell, *The Elders: Seniority in Earliest Christianity*, Edinburgh: T & T Clark, 1994).

Paul's letters to Timothy and Titus weren't called the "Pastoral Epistles" until around the eighteenth century. Timothy and Titus were not pastors as we conceive of them today. They were in Paul's circle of apostolic workers, usually on the move. On occasion they tarried in a single location. Significantly, Paul never calls them pastors or elders. He does call Timothy an "evangelist"....

My observation would be that the great bulk of people who have been sitting in pews hearing sermons for 30-50 years are rarely equipped for ministry, are often biblically illiterate, and are essentially trained to be ears for the mouth of the body—spoon-fed and dependent on the charisma of one gift behind the pulpit (*cf.* Clyde Reid, *The God-Evaders*, Harper, 1966; *The Empty Pulpit*, Harper, 1967)....

I think the following summary by Ernest F. Scott once again confirms that the pivotal points made in *PC* have been seen by others.

[The *ekklesia*] was not the Jewish community over again, with a few minor differences, but was a new creation.... [W]hen much of [Paul's] spiritual teaching was forgotten...the church took on more and more of the character of an ordinary society. It sought its models deliberately in the guilds and corporations of the day, and before a century had passed a Christian church was almost a replica in miniature of a Roman municipality. It had a body of officers graded like those of the city, clothed in similar vestments and bearing similar titles. The conception of a unique society, representing on earth the new order, which would prevail in the Kingdom, seemed almost to have disappeared (*The Nature of the Early Church*, Charles Scribner's Sons, 1941, pp. 31, 110).

Few would deny that the *agape* meal and multi-participant meetings are present in the NT. The crucial issue is, did they cease for valid reasons? Roman Catholic D.I. Lanslots freely admits (as he seeks to justify the RCC agenda):

The public worship or the Liturgy, which is a certain development of prayers and ceremonies, as we have it today, did not exist in the days of the Apostles.... Two early ceremonies, that accompanied the celebration [Holy Eucharist], soon disappeared; they were not essential. The first was the love-feast; the other the spiritual exercises, in which people were moved by the Holy Ghost to prophesy, speak in divers tongues, heal the sick by prayer, and so on; St. Paul in his first epistle to the Corinthians refers to that (*cf.* 14:1-14) [*The Primitive Church: The Church in the Days of the Apostles* [1926], Tan Books, 1980, pp. 264-265].

"They were not essential," he affirms. In terms of practice, Protestants have essentially agreed with this notion. *PC* is suggesting that what came in their place was substandard, contra the NT traditions, and ended up effectively redefining the NT concept of church....

Protestants usually affirm that the NT is the benchmark for all of life, and our life in the Body of Christ. As *PC* points out, the visible church began to takes it cue from traditions other than the NT quite early on. G. A. Jacob pointed out this phenomenon during a 19th century ecclesiastical struggle in his day:

> Notwithstanding the still generally acknowledged supremacy of Holy Scripture amongst us, the main current of Church opinion on all questions of polity and practice (to say nothing here of doctrines) has for a very considerable time been setting strongly towards the ecclesiastical system of the third and fourth centuries, to the neglect, in this respect, of the New Testament.... [The movement] was begun and carried on by men who diligently and perseveringly brought to bear upon the public mind their stores of learning, gathered not from the Apostles, but from the post-apostolic Fathers; not from the divinely taught Church of the New Testament, but from the humanly deteriorated Church of a later time.... And all the while there is frequently a profound ignorance of what the Church system at that time really was, and the extent to which it had departed from the simplicity of the apostolic age and truth (*The Ecclesiastical Polity of the New Testament: A study for the present crisis in the Church of England*, Thomas Whitaker, 1879, pp. 20-21, 23).

So it would seem that we really need to ask ourselves, "Do we take the revelation in the NT seriously as our starting point, and does the way we practice church honestly reflect NT values?" I think *PC* has done a marvelous job of challenging us to re-visit these questions as does the sequel, *Reimagining Church*.

— **Jon Zens**

SOURCES

USED IN RESEARCH & REFLECTION

» Donald R. Allen, *Barefoot in the Church: Sensing the Authentic Through the House Church*, John Knox Press, 1973, 188 pp.

» Tom Allen, *Congregations in Conflict*, Christian Publications, 1991, 176 pp.

» Randall Arthur, *Wisdom Hunter: A Novel*, Multnomah Publishers, 1992, 323 pp.

» Christopher Ash, *Listen Up! A Practical Guide to Listening to Sermons*, The Good Book Company, 2000, 30 pp.

» James M. Ault, Jr. "Marriage," *Spirit & Flesh: Life in a Fundamentalist Baptist Church*, Alfred A. Knopf, 2004, pp. 246-259.

» Francis O. Ayres, *The Ministry of the Laity: A Biblical Exposition*, The United Methodist Church, 1962, 139 pp.

» Steve Bagi, *Pastor Pain: My Journey in Burnout*, Actuate Consulting, 2008, 105 pp.

» Robert Banks, *Paul's Idea of Community—The Early House Churches in Their Historical Setting* (Eerdmans,1980) 208 pp.

» Pierre Berton, *The Comfortable Pew: A Critical Look at Christianity & the Religious Establishment in the New Age*, J.P. Lippincott, 1967, 137 pp.

» Samuel Bownas [1676-1753], *A Description of the Qualifications Necessary to A Gospel Minister*, Pendle Hill Publications, 1989, 104 pp.

» J.R. Boyd, *The Wood Chopper Preacher's Story*, self-published, 1980, 266 pp.

» Emil Brunner, *The Misunderstanding of the Church*, Lutterworth Press, 1952, 132 pp.

» Colin Bulley, *The Priesthood of Some Believers: Developments from the General to the Specific Priesthood in the Christian Literature of the First Three Centuries*, Paternoster Press, 2000, 336 pp.

» Donald Capps, *Pastoral Care: A Thematic Approach*, Westminster Press, 1979, 161 pp.

» Joel Carpenter, "Fundamentalist Institutions & the Rise of Evangelical Protestantism, 1929-1942," *American Church History: A Reader*, Henry W. Bowden & P.C. Kemeny, eds., Abingdon Press, 1988, pp. 390-400.

» Eugene Cho, "Death By Ministry," http://www.churchleaders.com/pastors/pastor-articles/146201-death-by-ministry.html.

» *Concern*. #17, February, 1969: (1) Walter Klaassen, "New Presbyter Is Old Priest Writ Large"; J. Lawrence Burkholder, "Theological Education for the Believer's Church"; John H. Yoder, "The Fullness of Christ."

» Mark D. Constantine, *Travelers on the Journey: Pastors Talk About Their Lives & Commitments*, Eerdmans, 2005, 220 pp.

» Kevin Craig, "Is the 'Sermon' Concept Biblical?" *Searching Together*, 15:1-2, Spring/Summer, 1986.

» Michael H. Crosby, *The Dysfunctional Church: Addiction & Codependency in the Family of Catholicism*, Ave Maria Press, 1991, 256 pp.

» Nancy DeMoss, *Potential Pitfalls of Ministry: Avoiding the Snares of Ministry*, cassette with study notes, Life Action Ministries, 2000.

» Richard Dortch, *Integrity: How I Lost It, and My Journey Back*, New Leaf Press, 1992, 350 pp.

» Michael Dwinell, *Being Priest to One Another*, Triumph Books, 1993, 198 pp.

» Jacques Ellul, *The Subversion of Christianity*, Eerdmans, 1986, 212 pp.

» Darryl Erkel, "The Urgent Need for Reformation in Pastoral Ministry," *Searching Together*, 36:1-2, Spring/Summer, 2009.

» Larry Eskridge & Mark A. Noll, *More Money, More Ministry: Money & Evangelicals in Recent North American History*, Eerdmans, 2000, 429 pp.

» Philip F. Esler, ed., *Modelling Early Christianity: Social-Scientific Studies of the New Testament in Its Context*, Routledge, 2004, 349 pp.

» Jack Fortenberry, *Corinthian Elders: "Knowledge makes arrogant but love edifies,"* self-published, 2005, 69 pp.

» Carl F. George with Warren Bird, *Nine Keys to Effective Small Group Leadership: How Lay Leaders Can Establish Dynamic & Healthy Cells, Classes, or Teams*, Kingdom Publishing, 1997, 216 pp.

» Robert Girard, "Reviving The Priesthood," 10:3 (Autumn, 1981) *Baptist Reformation Review*, pp. 31-37.

» Jim W. Goll, "The Separation of 'Clergy' & 'Laity,'" *Father, Forgive Us! Freedom from Yesterday's Sin*, Destiny Image, 1999, pp. 75-91.

» Joel Gregory, *Too Great A Temptation: The Seductive Power of America's Super Church*, The Summit Group, 1994, 332 pp.

» Craig Groeschel, *Confessions of a Pastor: Adventures in Dropping the Pose & Getting Real with God*, Multnomah Publishers, 2006, 221 pp.

» Mary Tuomi Hammond, *The Church & the Dechurched: Mending a Damaged Faith*, Chalice Press, 2001, 189pp.

» Hezekiah Harvey, *The Pastor: His Qualifications & Duties* [1879], Backus Book Publishers, 1982, 180 pp.

» William D. Hendricks, *Exit Interviews: Revealing Stories of Why People Are Leaving the Church*, Moody Press, 1993, 305 pp.

» Ronald F. Hock, *The Social Context of Paul's Ministry: Tentmaking & Apostleship*, Fortress Press, 1980, 112 pp.

» Greg Hufstetler, "The Support of Elders in the N.T.," 7:2 (Summer, 1978), *Baptist Reformation Review*.

» Ernest & Laequinia Hunter, *Ministry Shall Not Destroy My Marriage*, Kingdom Publishing Group, 2010, 100 pp.

» Anne Jackson, *Mad Church Disease: Overcoming the Burnout Epidemic*, Zondervan, 2009, 190 pp.

» Marion L. Jacobsen, *Crowded Pews & Lonely People*, Tyndale House Publishers, 1975, 207 pp.

» David Johnson & Jeff VanVonderen, *The Subtle Power of Spiritual Abuse: Recognizing & Escaping Spiritual Manipulation & False Spiritual Authority within the Church*, Bethany House Publishers, 1991, 234 pp.

» Jan G. Johnson, "Church Brawls," *Ministry*, November, 1990, pp. 17-19.

» J.H. Jowett, *The Preacher: His Life & Work*, Baker Book House, 1969, 239 pp.

» Barbara Kingsolver, *The Poisonwood Bible: A Novel*, HarperPerennial, 1999, 546 pp.

» David L. Larsen, *Caring for the Flock: Pastoral Ministry in the Local Congregation*, Crossway Books, 1991, 256 pp.

» Alan Lear, "Concerns About Traditional Ministry Patterns: An African Perspective," *Searching Together*, 24:4, Winter, 1996.

» H.B. London & Neil B. Wiseman, *Married to a Pastor's Wife: A Read-Together, Write-Together Book to Help Pastoral Couples Survive Ministry Risks*, Victor Books, 1995, 287 pp.

» Bruce J. Malina, *Christian Origins & Cultural Anthropology: Practical Models for Biblical Interpretation*, John Knox Press, 1986, 230 pp.

» Gary L. McIntosh & Samuel D. Rima, Sr., *Overcoming the Dark Side of Leadership: the Paradox of Personal Dysfunction*, Baker, 1997, 233 pp.

» Sidney E. Mead, "From Coercion to Persuasion: Another Look at the Rise of Religious Liberty & the Emergence of Denominationalism," *American Church History: A Reader*, Bowden/Kemeny, eds., Abingdon Press, 1988, pp. 243-255.

» Paul Miller, *Leading The Family of God* (Herald Press, 1981), 213 pp.

» David O. Moberg, *The Church as a Social Institution: The Sociology of American Religion*, Baker Book House, 2nd Edition, 1984, 602 pp.

» Jurgen Moltmann & Hans Kung, eds., *Who Has the Say in the Church? Concilium: Religion in the Eighties*, The Seabury Press, 1981, 86 pp.

» R. Lawrence Moore, *Selling God: American Religion in the Marketplace of Culture*, Oxford University Press, 1994, 317 pp.

» Ian Murray, "The Christian Ministry & the Challenge to Its Continuance," *Banner of Truth*, Issue 237, June, 1983, pp.6-10, 12; "The Christian Ministry & the Challenge to Its Continuance #2," *Banner of Truth*, Issue 238, July, 1983, pp. 1-5.

» Henri J.M. Nouwen, *In the Name of Jesus: Reflections on Christian Leadership*, The Crossroad Publishing Co., 1990, 81 pp.

» Larry Osborne, *Sticky Teams: Keeping Your Leadership Team & Staff on the Same Page*, Zondervan, 2009, 224 pp.

» Carolyn Osiek & David L. Balch, *Families in the New Testament World: Households & House Churches*, Westminster/John Knox Press, 1997, 329 pp.

» Elaine Pagels, "One God, One Bishop: The Politics of Monotheism," *The Gnostic Gospels*, Vintage Books, 1989. pp. 28-47.

» J. Edgar Park, "The Miracle of Preaching" [Book Condensation], *Pulpit Digest*, December, 1956, 37:224, pp. 95-114.

» Mike Parker, "The Basic Meaning of 'Elder' in the N.T.;" Vol.7 #2 (Summer, 1978), *Baptist Reformation Review*.

» Stephen Parsons, *Ungodly Fear: Fundamentalist Christianity & the Abuse of Power*, Lion Publishing, 2000, 320 pp.

» Dorothy Harrison Pentecost, *The Pastor's Wife & the Church*, Moody Press, 9th printing, 1979, 315 pp.

» John Piper, *Brothers, We Are Not Professionals: A Plea to Pastors for Radical Ministry*, Broadman & Holman, 2002, 286 pp.

» James N. Poling, *The Abuse of Power: A Theological Problem*, Abingdon Press, 1991, 224 pp.

» David Prior, *Jesus & Power*, InterVarsity Press, 1988, 192 pp.

» Soong-Chan Rah, *The Next Evangelicalism: Freeing the Church from Western Cultural Captivity*, InterVarsity Press, 2009, 229 pp.

» Robert L. Randall, *Pastor & Parish: The Psychological Core of Ecclesiastical Conflicts*, Human Sciences Press, 1988, 172 pp.

» Thomas C. Reeves, *The Empty Church: Does Organized Religion Matter Anymore?* Touchstone, 1996, 276 pp.

» Cylde Reid, *The Empty Pulpit*, Harper & Row, 1967, 122 pp.

» Clyde Reid, *The God-Evaders*, Harper & Row, 1966, 118 pp.

» Larry Richards and Clyde Hoeldtke. *A Theology of Church Leadership* (Zondervan, 1980), 399 pp.

» Larry Richards and Gene Getz. "A Biblical Style of Leadership?" *Leadership*, Spring Quarter, 1981, pp. 68-70. (A friendly debate, which focuses on two ways of looking at leadership in the church: [1] the focus on the pastor as a source of leadership [Getz], and [2] the focus on elders as leaders within the decision making process of the body [Richards]).

» Larry Richards and Gib Martin, *A Theology of Personal Ministry*, Zondervan.

» Adrian Rogers, "Depression in the Ministry," message given at the Rapha luncheon at the Southern Baptist Convention, 1989 video.

» Anne Rowthorn, *The Liberation of the Laity*, Morehouse Publishing, 1990, 141 pp.

» John A. Sanford, *Ministry Burnout*, Paulist Press, 1982, 117 pp.

» Dan Schaeffer, *Faking Church: The Subtle Deflection*, Barbour Publishing, 2004, 255pp.

» Edward Schillebeeckx, *Ministry: Leadership in the Community of Jesus Christ*, The Crossroad Publishing Company, 1981, 165 pp.

» Judy Schindler, "The Rise of One-Bishop Rule in the Early Church," *Baptist Reformation Review*, 10:2, Summer, 1981.

» David S. Schuller, Merton P. Strommen & Milo L. Brekke, eds., *Ministry in America: A Report & Analysis, Based on an In-Depth Survey of 47 Denominations in the United States & Canada*, with Interpretation by 18 Experts, Harper & Row, 1980, 582 pp.

» Norman Shawchuck & Roger Heuser, *Leading the Congregation: Caring for Yourself While Serving Others*, Abingdon Press, 1993, 339 pp.

» "Shelly Speaks with 'Pastor' John About His Sermon Last Sunday," http://www.youtube.com/watch?v=WQ34Nl-XZRQ

» Howard A. Snyder with Daniel V. Runyon, "From Clergy/Laity to Community of Ministers," *Foresight: 10 Major Trends that Will Dramatically Affect the Future of Christians & the Church*, Thomas Nelson Publishers, 1986, 190 pp.

» Ralph W. Sockman, "What Is Real in Church?" *Pulpit Digest*, December, 1956, 37:224, pp. 27-34.

» Josh Spencer, "Christianity Deconstructed #2: The Preaching of Sermons," www.strangerthingsmag.com, November, 2000.

» Bruce Stabbert, *The Team Concept: Paul's Church Leadership or Ours?* Hegg Brothers Printing, 1982, 226 pp.

» Wolfgang Stegemann, Bruce J. Malina & Gerd Theissen, eds., *The Social Setting of Jesus & the Gospels*, Fortress Press, 2002, 404 pp.

» Melvin J. Steinbron, *Can the Pastor Do It Alone: A Model for Preparing Lay People for Lay Pastoring*, Regal Books, 1987, 258 pp.

» Stanley Stuber, *How We Got Our Denominations: A Primer on Church History*, Association Press, 1948, 224 pp.

» Ron Susek, *Firestorm: Preventing & Overcoming Church Conflicts*, Baker, 1999, 252 pp.

» Jeremy Thomson, *Preaching as Dialogue: Is the Sermon a Sacred Cow?*, Grove Books Limited, 1996, 24 pp.

» Ronald Tobin, *Every One A Minister* (e-book)

» Stefan Ulstein, *Pastors [Off the Record]: Straight Talk About Life in the Ministry*, InterVarsity Press, 1993, 246 pp.

» Frank Viola & George Barna, *Pagan Christianity: Exploring the Roots of Our Church Practices*, Tyndale, 2008, 336 pp.

» Frank Viola, *Reimagining Church: Pursuing the Dream of Organic Christianity*, David C. Cook, 2008, 320pp.

» Norbert Ward, "Who Has Authority in the Church?" 5:2 (Summer, 1976), *Baptist Reformation Review*, pp. 22-23.

» Marjorie Warkentin, *Ordination: A Biblical & Historical Study*, Eerdmans 1982, 202 pp.

» Ronald W. Wiebe & Bruce A. Rowlison, *Let's Talk About Church Staff Relationships*, Green Leaf Press, 1983, 60 pp.

» Paul Wilkes, "The Hands That Would Shape Our Souls: the changing and often deeply troubled world of America's Protestant, Catholic & Jewish seminaries," *The Atlantic Monthly*, December, 1990, pp. 59-88.

» Don Williams, *Jesus & Addiction: A Prescription to Transform the Dysfunctional Church & Recover Authentic Christianity*, Recovery Publications, 1993, 197 pp.

» Ben Witherington III, "Neither Clergy Nor Laity—A New Testament Vision of Ministry," Lecture given in Houston, TX, February, 2010, http://blog.beliefnet.com/bibleandculture/2010/02/neither-clergy-nor-laity---a-nt-vision-of-ministry.html.

» John Howard Yoder, "The Fullness of Christ," *Searching Together*, 11:3, Autumn, 1982.

» John Howard Yoder, "The Hermeneutics of Peoplehood: A Protestant Perspective," *The Priestly Kingdom*, University of Notre Dame Press, 1985, pp. 15-45.

» Jon Zens, *A Church Building Every ½ Mile: What Makes American Christianity Tick?* Ekklesia Press, 2008, 126 pp.

AFTERWORD

Reading this book revived many memories of my past. Just yesterday, I received a "humorous" email from a clergy friend, offering a tried and true "blueprint" for the arrangement of a pastor's desk. I laughed out loud; here was an excellent reminder of where I have come from. For almost thirty-five years as a pastor in a large conservative denomination, my office desk contained each of the items on that blueprint, along with all the various stacks of files and papers, arranged in varying configurations over the years. Four years ago, however, I had grown deeply troubled by the "disconnect" between what that blueprint represented and the New Testament pictures of life and ministry in the early churches. I resigned, not just from the churches I was serving as a pastor, but from the pastoral office and from the denomination to which I had dedicated the first sixty years of my life.

Initially, believing that this contrast was primarily a problem within my own denomination, which I had not been able to see because of cultural myopia, my wife, Bonnie, and I began a search for a church we could call home. We were looking for a gathering of God's people where the vitality of Christ Jesus was involving all His people in sharing, worship and activity of ministry. Unfortunately, we floundered for some time; there seemed to be no church or denomination with a clear perception of that living organism, which Jesus has established as His church. We have certainly met many wonderful, committed disciples of Jesus in this search, but the structure and approach of a clergy-formatted blueprint always seemed to stifle the lively, spontaneous activity of the Lord in and among His people in each instance.

Our God, however, is faithful in keeping His promises. I'm certain that the original hearers of Jesus' words, "Seek and ye shall find," could not even have begun to envision the computer or Internet. My wife, though, in faithful persistence, used that wonderful tool to locate a group of faithful believers in Omaha,

NE, who had been on a similar journey to our own. Through them, we were made aware of Jon Zens and the print ministry of *Searching Together*. What a "find" that has been for us!

For over thirty years, Jon has been addressing many of the very same concerns that were troubling to us. With thorough and intense study of the Scriptures, an honest look at history and a deep faith in Jesus as the Lord of the church, he has written with clarity about many of the difficulties that have resulted from the unbiblical "clergy/laity" distinction in the church. Along with this identification of the negative, however, he has consistently stressed the Scriptural positive, issuing a clarion call for a return of all God's people to full involvement in the life and ministry of the local gatherings of the church, the *ekklesia*.

I have been eagerly awaiting this volume, which brings together Jon's insights from past to present in his searching and journey related to the "clergy/laity" distinction in the church. Life in God's Kingdom, after all is never static. The Holy Spirit continues to reveal and unveil the clear truths of the Scriptures to His people. Studying together, sharing together, praying together provide a wonderful culture for those truths to be made more clear. I have had the privilege of doing all of that with Jon and can testify that he humbly and seriously seeks to live out what he teaches and believes. The insights unfolded in this volume have challenged me, inspired me, encouraged me and sometimes bothered and irritated me. The result, though, is that I have been helped to be reoriented to the *ekklesia* that breathes the life of Jesus in and through all of its members. This book truly enacts the very thing it proclaims: the sharing of the "one another" encouragements, which predominate in the New Testament. This is exactly what is needed in the churches and among the people of God in our generation.

— **Gary Jaeckle**
Diagonal, Iowa

ACKNOWLEDGEMENTS

Special thanks to the following people who contributed their expertise to this project: Wilma Bell, Kathy Huff, Gordon Gillesby, Patricia Gillesby, Bonnie Jaeckle, Rafael Polendo, Jodi Root, Abigail Wolfer, and Graham Wood (UK). Hats off to Graham who spent many hours editing the three older articles and then turned them into edited Word documents!

 *Ekklesia Press*

Ekklesia Press offers books to develop and encourage believers to be God's Ekklesia: His called out who live within an unbelieving world. Our productions have a prophetic edge. They will challenge you, uproot empty tradition and help you to live the kingdom of God in conjunction to others who realize the Kingdom of God is not just an eventuality.

The Diluted Church
Calling Believers To Live Out Of Their True Heritage
by Timothy L. Price *(June 2005)*

Christ in Y'all
Following Jesus Into Community
by Neil Carter *(August 2008)*

NEW THIS YEAR!

The Spirituality of Discontent
Reflections on the Sermon on the Mount
By Bong Manayon *(due out: Spring 2011)*

Also available from Jon Zens...

What's With Paul And Women?
Unlocking the Cultural Background to
1 Timothy 2
(2010)

A Church Building Every 1/2 Mile
What Makes American Christianity Tick?
(2008)

PRE-EKKLESIA PUBLISHED

"This Is My Beloved Son, Hear Him":
The Foundation for New Covenant Ethics & Ecclesiology
Searching Together, 1997

Moses & the Millennium:
An Appraisal of Christian Reconstructionism
Searching Together, 1988

Desiring Unity...Finding Division:
Lessons from the 19th Century Restorationist Movement
Searching Together, 1986

The above are available at www.jonzens.com

CPSIA information can be obtained at www.ICGtesting.com
Printed in the USA
237804LV00001B/53/P